BOOST YOUR MIND POWER week by week

BOOST YOUR MIND POWER week by week

Bill Lucas

52 techniques to make you smarter

DUNCAN BAIRD PUBLISHERS

LONDON

Boost Your Brain Power Week by Week
Bill Lucas

Distributed in the USA and Canada by
Sterling Publishing Co., Inc.
387 Park Avenue South
New York, NY 10016-8810

This edition first published in the UK and USA in 2006 by
Duncan Baird Publishers Ltd
Sixth Floor, Castle House
75–76 Wells Street
London W1T 3QH

Copyright © Duncan Baird Publishers 2006
Text copyright © Bill Lucas 2006
Artwork copyright © Duncan Baird Publishers 2006

Mind Maps® are a registered trademark to Tony Buzan in the UK and US.

The right of Bill Lucas to be identified as the Author of this text has been asserted in accordance with the Copyright, Designs and Patents Act of 1988.

All rights reserved. No part of this book may be reproduced in any form or by any electronic or mechanical means, including information storage and retrieval systems, without permission in writing from the publisher, except by a reviewer who may quote brief passages in a review.

Managing Editor: Caroline Ball
Editor: Zoë Stone
Managing Designer: Daniel Sturges
Designer: Clare Thorpe
Commissioned Illustrations: ichapel.co.uk

Library of Congress Cataloging-in-Publication Data is available
ISBN: 978-1-84483-264-4

10 9 8 7 6 5 4 3

Typeset in Ehrhardt and Franklin Gothic
Color reproduction by Colourscan, Singapore
Printed in Malaysia for Imago

Publisher's note: Neither the Publisher nor the Author can accept responsibility for any injuries or damage incurred as a result of following the health advice in this book.

For information about custom editions, special sales, premium and corporate purchases, please contact Sterling Special Sales Department at 800-805-5489 or specialsales@sterlingpub.com.

Contents

Introduction

Have you ever stopped to think what is going on when you are using your mind? What's happening inside your head when you are thinking of solutions to a problem, trying to remember someone's name or learning a new skill? If you knew the answers to these questions, then you would be getting closer to understanding the most extraordinary and wonderful part of you – your mind.

For much of the 18th and 19th centuries it was widely believed that our brains are like empty vessels waiting to be filled up with facts. But thinking has moved on since then. With the advent of modern brain scanning and imaging techniques, we have begun to realize that emotions are just as important as facts.

We have begun to understand the ways in which we are all very different. We have begun to see that intelligence is not fixed, that we can learn to be smarter. And that an awareness of our mindset and the way we choose to go about a task enables us to get more and more out of our minds.

For hundreds of years children have been taught the 3 Rs of Reading, wRiting and aRithmetic. But, valuable as these are, they will not ensure that you are able to deal with the complex challenges of the century we live in. In this book I offer you instead my own prescription for boosting your mind power, the 5 Rs:

Resourcefulness, Resilience, Remembering, Reflectiveness and Responsiveness. Resourcefulness is having a range of techniques at your finger tips for every situation. Resilience is the ability to know what to do when you are stuck. Remembering is the capacity to use what you have learned before in new situations. Reflectiveness is extracting meaning from living. And Responsiveness involves putting what you have learned into practice, changing and adapting as you go.

Equipped with my 5 Rs, I believe anyone has the potential to be happy and successful in a fast-changing world. But the key to realizing this potential is you: you have to want to improve and be prepared to put time and effort into doing so.

In the 21st century, the capacity to learn well will be an invaluable skill and the most important organ you have to help you is your mind. The 52 steps in this book will show you a whole host of ways in which you can give your mind a good work-out. You might like to try one new technique each week. Or you might prefer to browse in a more leisurely fashion, or go on a fitness binge and have a go at lots of techniques at once. Nearly every step includes signposts (just look for the ➤➤ icon at the bottom of the page) which direct you to other relevant steps. Whichever approach you take, this book will show you how you can learn how to learn more effectively for the rest of your life.

CHAPTER 1

How Your Mind Works

In the past 20 years great strides have been made in understanding some of the complexities of the human brain, although there are still many aspects of it that are only partially understood. But how we remember, how we communicate information and feelings to others, our ability to persist in a task or make good decisions involves much more than engaging a particular collection of brain cells. We may not be aware of it but we are also involving our innate characteristics, our past experiences and our outside influences – our whole mind.

So what is our mind? Put very simply, it is brain plus personality. One of the key tricks to boosting your mind power is to capitalize on your strengths and recognize and build on your weaknesses. Later in the book, we'll see how this can be done in more detail, but first you might like to do a little self-analysis, to find out what sort of mind you have and how it likes to operate.

1 Different Kinds of Smart

When Dr Howard Gardner, a professor of cognition and education at Harvard University, suggested the idea of multiple intelligences in the 1980s, he started a revolution. Before this, intelligence was almost entirely judged in relation to IQ. Tests covered mathematical and linguistic skills, with a bit of problem-solving thrown in for good measure. While IQ tests effectively sifted academic individuals from those who were more practical by nature, they were a poor indicator of future success in life, love or work. They also provided a very limited definition of what it was to be smart.

Gardner's idea is remarkably simple and it goes with the grain of common sense. He identified eight types of intelligence, which I have described below (with Gardner's original names in brackets if they were different). The final two types on the list have been added by other thinkers since Gardner developed his theory. See if you can recognize yourself in any or some of these descriptions.

Linguistic

You like words and stories. Word-play intrigues you and you are an avid reader. You have a good vocabulary. You probably enjoy learning languages. You like writing and may well be able to remember lists of words and tell good stories.

Mathematical (Logical-mathematical)

You seek to understand the relationships between different things. You like figures, abstract problems, brain-teasers and puzzles. You appreciate patterns, categories and systems. You probably make lists.

Visual (Spatial)

You notice colour, form and texture. You probably use pictures to help you remember things, and diagrams, maps and doodles when you are making notes. You may well be able to draw, paint or sculpt.

Physical (Bodily-kinesthetic)

You enjoy physical exercise, sports and dance. You tend to be on your feet at the first opportunity whether in a meeting or at a party. You learn by rolling up your sleeves and getting on with things.

Musical

You are attuned to sounds and rhythms. You probably relished singing and listening to music from an early age. You can recall songs and melodies well. Music impacts powerfully on your moods.

Emotional (Intrapersonal)

You tend to look within yourself, on a constant quest for self-knowledge. You may keep a diary of your experiences, moods and thoughts. You enjoy time to think and reflect, and you understand and manage your own emotions well.

Social (Interpersonal)

You enjoy other people's company and getting to know people. Parties, meetings, team games and gregarious activities appeal to your nature. You show high levels of empathy with other people.

Environmental (Naturalist)

You are fascinated by nature, and see things in it that pass others by. You probably like being outdoors and are fond of animals. You take a keen interest in your home environment, inside and outside.

Spiritual

You enjoy grappling with the fundamental questions of existence. You tend to act according to your principles, possibly questioning the normal ways of behaving in a given situation. You probably hold well-developed beliefs that you are ready to stand up for.

Practical

You like making things happen. You are often called on to fix, mend or assemble things, or to come up with solutions. Where others talk about what needs to be done, you prefer to get on and do it.

EXERCISE: Develop All Your Talents

Intelligence is not fixed. While you may not become a Mozart or an Einstein, you can improve on your current capacity. Use a chart like the one below to assess your own multiple intelligences. For each type of intelligence, decide whether you have high, medium or low amounts of it at the moment. Then use the third column for ideas for developing that intelligence. I have given you a few examples to get you started.

Intelligence	High, medium, low	Ideas for developing the intelligence
Linguistic	*Low*	*Join a book club, learn a language*
Mathematical		
Visual		
Physical	*Medium*	*Learn how to dance*
Musical		
Emotional	*Low*	*Keep a diary, take up meditation*
Social		
Environmental	*Medium*	*Learn garden design*
Spiritual		
Practical		

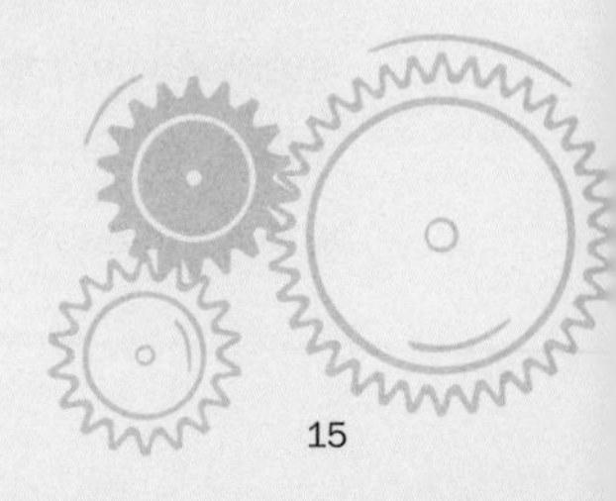

2 Your Learning Style

We don't leave learning behind when we leave school, college or university. At many times in our lives we find we need to learn new things, whether they are academic or practical. And we all apply our minds to problems or react to circumstances in different ways.

About a hundred years ago the Swiss psychologist Carl Jung developed a theory about personality. He argued that the differences we see in those around us are the result of preferences relating to our fundamental personalities. Jung's theory has been developed by Katharine Cook Briggs and Isabel Briggs Myers.

Common traits in different Types

Take a look at the Myers Briggs Type Indicator® (MBTI) opposite. Can you pick out the Type or Types that most seem to describe you? It's often easier to see traits in other people rather than yourself, so ask someone to "analyze" you, and try to identify the Types of some members of your family or people with whom you work, too. Think about how they approach different types of learning, problems, and so on. Do people who are a similar Type use similar methods or approaches? Do they do things differently from you? If so, you might be able to follow their example. We can all learn from seeing how somebody of a similar Type deals with something successfully.

The Myers Briggs Type Indicator® (MBTI)

- **Extroverts** tend to be sociable, enjoy interaction and work things out as they go along. They like variety and love to give their opinion. **Introverts** gain energy from inside, tend to have a small number of deep relationships, and think carefully before speaking. They are good listeners who keep their thoughts to themselves.
- **Sensors** gather information in an exact and sequential manner and tend to be realistic, down-to-earth and specific. They go for facts and details and like to know how things work. **Intuitives** are more likely to gather information in an imprecise, big picture sort of a way, relying on hunches and staying alert to possibilities.
- **Thinkers** take decisions in an impartial, fair-minded way. They are detached, logical and firm, like to know they are taking the right decision and enjoy offering constructive criticism. **Feelers** take decisions in a collaborative and subjective way. Other people's feelings matter to them and they are unwilling to upset people if they can possibly avoid it.
- **Judgers** tend toward an attitude to life that is fixed, controlled and planned with tight deadlines. They like making lists and making sure they finish things. **Perceivers** have a wait and see attitude, they are adaptable, flexible and open-ended. They prefer starting to finishing things.

A widely used alternative of the MBTI® was created by Peter Honey and Alan Mumford. It draws on the work of David Kolb. They suggested four distinct types of learning styles:

- **Activists** tend to immerse themselves in experiences and will try anything once. They thrive on the excitement of the here and now and are easily bored.
- **Pragmatists** like methods that encourage them to work on real issues where they can see an obvious practical benefit. They recognize that constraints are inevitable.
- **Reflectors** enjoy having time to stand back, think and ponder. They dislike having to give instant responses.
- **Theorists** like a clear underlying concept or model to follow. They choose methodical approaches and tend not to like taking part in open-ended activities.

Which type rings most true for you? Understanding which type or types you are will help you find the best way of applying your mind to a new situation. If you cannot immediately work it out, see which of these statements most describes your instinctive reaction:

"I'll try anything once" (Activist)

"There must be a better way" (Pragmatist)

"I'll need to think about that one" (Reflector)

"But how does that fit in with...?" (Theorist)

EXERCISE: Extend Your Learning Style

Whatever your learning type, you will find learning easier if you work out the answers to the following:

Learning situations	Things to try
Where do you like to learn? At home? At work? When commuting? In a library or museum? In some kind of educational institution or in a social setting?	Start by going to places you feel most comfortable in, and then try incorporating new places – changing location can sometimes provide a helpful new perspective.
What is your ideal learning environment? Quiet or noisy? With or without music? In an easy chair or at a desk?	Take control of your personal learning environment and don't feel put off by others.
When do you like to learn?	Choose your most alert times when you have important brain work!
How do you like to learn? By giving it a go? Reading books? Watching others? Doing Research? Keeping a diary? Listening or talking with others? Role-playing? Using computers? In carefully structured situations or in practical situations?	When you find a subject difficult, choose a method you prefer and you know works well for you. But gradually try to extend your range. Experimenting with different methods can help the learning process.

3 How You Learn

As you learn, huge amounts of data are entering your brain via your five senses. Meanwhile, inside your brain some 100 billion nerve cells are processing this. Each time a nerve cell (or neuron) connects with another, an electrical and chemical exchange takes place and the beginning of a memory is stored.

So how does this work in practice? A useful model, sometimes credited to W.C. Howell, describes the process for learning a new skill as a sequence from unconscious incompetence to unconscious competence. This model applies well to something like learning to drive. First you do not even know you want to drive. Then you decide you want to, but realize you don't know how. When you begin learning you need to concentrate hard on every aspect and use reminders such as "mirror, signal, manoeuvre". Then one day you suddenly find that you have changed gear without even noticing.

Any kind of learning inevitably involves dealing with the unknown, and this can be intimidating as it requires you to step outside your comfort zone. But the good news is that we learn best when we are operating at the edge of where we feel comfortably competent. And there's no need to panic! In this book I am going to show you how to confront and overcome the anxieties that accompany the prospect of learning.

EXERCISE: Recognize the Learning Sequence

Learning can be split into three aspects: the model (what you want to achieve), the strategies and reflection. Have a go at doing this for yourself with something specific you have recently achieved. It might be academic in nature (mastering a type of foreign-language verb), or physical (improving your tennis serve) or practical (pruning an apple tree correctly). Think back to the route you took and how it fits into the pattern described above. Use the following prompts to help you.

1. What was your aim?
2. What strategies worked well for you? (Repetitive practice? Classes or coaching? Working it out on your own or working with others?)
3. What else did you discover along the way? (Some methods that don't work well for you? An interest in taking the subject further? Added confidence?)

Keep a record (as a list, a plan or diagram or orally on to a tape), especially of all your reflections on what you learned about learning, so that you can apply them in other situations in future.

➤➤ Step 1: Different Kinds of Smart; Step 4: Using Your Senses; Step 10: Worst-case Scenarios; Step 16: Taking Stock; Step 17: Mistakes Are Good; Step 27: Know-how and Knowledge Transfer

4 Using Your Senses

How many senses do you have? The conventional answer is five, although some people think that intuition is a good candidate for a sixth!

Our senses are the antennae of our minds. With them we take in data to be processed and, where appropriate, stored as memories. In today's world sight and hearing are arguably the most crucial of the five. But the other three are important, too. With touch, taste and smell we stimulate emotions (which affect the effectiveness with which our mind is working) and access memory. Think of the way a powerful smell of polish can take you back to your school days or the taste of a special food can trigger the memory of a holiday when you first tasted it.

Although sight and hearing dominate, we might use a combination of any two or more senses for the way we take in data. Inventing a new recipe, say, relies heavily on the close-knit senses of taste and smell. And when you play a game with young children your mind might be constantly drawing on all your senses to think of ways of both amusing them and stimulating their minds.

➤➤Step 22: Visualization; Step 23: Using Your Intuition; Step 29: Making It Stick; Step 33: Feelings Matter

Sensory preferences are sometimes mistakenly described as learning styles. This suggests that they are somehow fixed, which they are not. Rather, as we grow up we tend to develop habits that engage one sense over another. For example, do you tend to listen to the news on the radio, or read it in a newspaper?

However, research suggests that we learn more effectively and improve our memory when we engage more than one sense. So, it is worth trying to go with the grain of what you like while at the same time trying to expand your repertoire.

EXERCISE: **Broadening Your Senses**

Think of all the activities that are engaging your mind. Identify which senses you are currently using and then move on to think of ways in which you could engage your other senses. I've given you some examples to get you started.

Activity	Senses being used	Ideas for using more of your senses
Reading	*Sight*	*Listen to a talking book, to sharpen your ability to take things in aurally*
Calming yourself	*Smell (aromatherapy candles and oils)*	*Touch (stress balls, worry beads)*
A cryptic crossword	*Sight*	*Hearing (listening to the sound of the words as you say them aloud can reveal other meanings or emphases)*

5 Staying Healthy in Mind and Body

Throughout this book you will find lots of different suggestions for improving the way you think, but each of them is only effective if your body is being treated well enough, too. Look after yourself by ensuring your diet is nutritious, you are well-hydrated and are getting enough sleep and exercise.

As well as your physical state, you need to consider your overall well-being. Are you warm enough? Safe enough? Feeling happy about yourself? If not, then your mind will find it difficult to work at its best. Use the following checklist to assess yourself, and think about ways you can improve the profile it comes up with.

CHECKLIST: **Health Check**	Seldom	Sometimes	Very often
Your body			
Do you exercise? *Take some kind of exercise every day (walking is fine).* *Do more vigorous exercise once or twice a week.*			
Do you eat plenty of foods that are high in antioxidants and foods that contain essential fatty acids (EFAs)? *Eat more richly coloured fruit and vegetables, and oily fish (or take fatty oil supplements), nuts and seeds.*			

	Seldom	Sometimes	Very often
Do you drink plenty of water, at least 1 litre every day? Do you drink more than 1 cup of coffee a day and/or a lot of tea or sugary drinks? *Try to drink 6 to 8 glasses of water a day. Tea and coffee are diuretics, so they will increase your need for fluids. Too much sugar can affect your mood and your health.*			
Do you wake up feeling refreshed? *Try training yourself to go to bed an hour earlier than you currently do.*			
Your mind			
Are you curious about life? *See Step 20: How to Ask Good Questions.*			
Are you confident about your memory? *See Chapter 5: Improving Your Memory.*			
Do you feel good about yourself? *See Chapters 2, 6 and Step 48: Good Stress, Bad Stress.*			
Do you set yourself clear goals? *See Step 51: Setting Goals.*			
Do you stick at things? *See Step 13: Keeping Going.*			
Do you feel too worried to concentrate? *See Step 8: Overcoming Barriers, Step 12: Concentration.*			

Mindset Matters

Mindset matters. To use your mind effectively you need first to be in the right frame of mind. Stop and recall moments when you have tried to read a map when you are angry or lost, or concentrate on instructions when you are feeling distressed. It's difficult when you are fighting negative emotions.

In this chapter you will learn how to take control of your emotions in order to become focused, proficient and happy in all that you do. By changing the attitudes of your mind, you can change day-to-day aspects of your life.

You will discover that the most conducive state for your mind to work well is one of relaxed alertness, and you will learn techniques for achieving this mindset. You will also find out how you can develop more positive, can-do attitudes to utilize your mind power. By contrast you will be able to banish those counterproductive states of mind and unhelpful habits which hinder your ability to learn.

At the end of this chapter I will share my unique model of learning with you – Ready, Go, Steady.

6 Relaxed Alertness

There is a particular state in which you will get the best out of your mind. In this condition you are both relaxed and alert. Bulgarian professor of psychiatry and psychotherapy Dr Georgi Lozanov is credited with first identifying this combination of states in the 1960s. He saw that you need to be alert enough to arouse your brain so that it becomes engaged, yet relaxed enough that you are in a receptive mood for learning, that you're not agitated or too stressed. In short, you need to be able to pay attention when you want to.

If you are not feeling very alert, then playing some lively music, stretching your legs with a brisk walk or just taking a break from what you are doing will often help. Try keeping to this simple guide: break every hour for a few minutes, every day for 20 minutes, every week for several hours, every month for at least two days, every year for at least two weeks.

However, in this fast-moving and increasingly busy world, it is likely that you will need to concentrate more on relaxing. There are two aspects to relaxing: the physical – unwinding your body; and the mental – practising the kinds of habits of mind that are likely to calm you down. The next exercises should help you do both.

➤➤Step 12: Concentration

EXERCISE 1: Relax Your Body

This exercise aims to reduce tension in the neck, back and larger muscles.

Find a quiet spot. Sit in a comfortable chair with your hands resting on your lap. Close your eyes. Take three deep, slow breaths. Then take yourself on a tour of your body and all its muscles. Start with your feet, then move up to your calves, then your knees, and so on, until you reach your neck. Then move down to your fingers and back up to your head, and finally down to your feet again. As you reach each part of your body, be aware of it and consciously try to relax and soften it. When you have finished, open your eyes slowly.

EXERCISE 2: Calm Your Mind

A short, regular period of meditation, say five or 10 minutes every day, can relax your mind in the same way that the exercise above relaxes your muscles.

Sit comfortably, with your back upright – you can kneel or sit cross-legged on a cushion, or sit on a hardback chair. You may like to have a candle flame or a familiar object to focus on. Let your hands relax in your lap. Gently sway to one side then the other three times, and then settle into stillness. Allow your thoughts to rise. Don't concentrate on them or ask yourself questions like "Why?" Maintain your stillness and your focus and envisage your thoughts rising and drifting away.

7 Being Half Full

Are you a "glass half full" or a "glass half empty" sort of person? Do you tend to emphasize positive aspects of a situation or point out what is likely to go wrong? Try this simple test. For each scenario, gauge the likelihood of it happening to you within the next year as a percentage. If a scenario is not applicable to you, choose something equivalent rather than scoring 0 percent:

1. Someone tells you how much they like you
2. You are praised for having a good idea
3. Someone compliments you on how attractive you look
4. You get a promotion at work
5. You win something
6. You meet someone special
7. You really enjoy your next vacation
8. You make a meal which everyone enjoys
9. You successfully find your way around an unfamiliar city
10. You buy someone a present which they really like.

Add up your total and divide it by 10 to get your final score.

0–40 You seem pessimistic
60–100 You seem optimistic
41–59 You are somewhere in between. Ask a friend to rate you!

Just as important as your score is whether you *think* of yourself as an optimist or a pessimist. And, more importantly, do you think it matters? (It does!)

In fact, research suggests that optimists generally do better in life, live longer and fulfill more of their ambitions. A study by the Mayo Clinic in the USA over a 30-year period has discovered that optimists live 19 percent longer than pessimists. Of course, optimists will tend to get things wrong more often, but making mistakes is all part of the learning curve. And crucially, optimists are less likely to give up. Cultivating a positive mindset will help your mind work better and help you achieve more.

Pessimists tend to:	Optimists tend to:
Lose heart easily	Be more resilient
Become depressed if things go wrong	Focus on solving the problem at hand
Make others feel gloomy	Be less stressed or anxious
Act as a drain on other people's energy	Inspire others to lift their performance

In his book *Learned Optimism: How to Change Your Mind And Your Life*, Dr Martin Seligman suggests that being optimistic or pessimistic stems from your "explanatory style" – the way you account for things that happen to you. He has described this as the

3 Ps: Permanence, Pervasiveness and Personalization. Let's look at each of the 3 Ps in turn.

Permanence: following a bad experience a pessimist might say "Things will never get better." But things seldom last for ever, even if it may seem so at times. Try to avoid using words like "always" and "never". An optimist might say "This is a temporary setback, tomorrow is a new day." Get into the habit of assuming that you are just having a bad day.

Pervasiveness: a pessimist will see an upset or setback spreading right through their lives, affecting everything. It is all too easy to generalize: one minute you miss your train, and the next you catch yourself complaining that trains are always late. An optimist will look on a setback as an isolated situation. Try to stop yourself making sweeping generalizations.

Personalization: when something goes wrong pessimists tend to blame themselves, sink into a depression, feel victimized and see a pattern of failure and bad luck. An optimist takes control of events and says "How can I get around this?" Stop blaming yourself and practise thinking of all the possible external causes instead.

The 3 Ps help to explain why people who seem to be very similarly gifted can have very different approaches toward handling a situation. The good news is that you can learn how to adopt a different mindset and see the world through a positive window.

TECHNIQUE: Develop a Positive Mindset – from 3 Ps to 3 Cs

The more aware you become about yourself, the more you can challenge your apparent beliefs and begin to think more positively. Think of something you found daunting or something that has recently gone wrong in your life. How did you explain this particular event? Is this typical of the way you view the world? If your explanation seems largely pessimistic, try to reframe it. Using the ideas on pages 31–32, make up statements which accentuate the positive, argue back at your pessimistic self and come up with alternative explanations. To help you with this, each of these approaches uses the letter C.

- **C**hange **C**an'ts to **C**ans: So, "I can't possibly cook a meal – no one will like my food" becomes "Of course I can cook supper."
- Argue your **C**ase: The next time something goes wrong, rather than falling into pessimistic mode, take issue with what you seem to be thinking. Instead of accepting your excuses, dispute them. Remind yourself that it is only a temporary issue, that it's a one-off and you are not to blame!
- **C**ome up with alternatives: It's easy to slip into patterns of behaviour. But if you have some alternatives you can begin to think differently. So whenever you find yourself with apparently only one explanation or one course of action, see if you can generate some possible alternatives.

➤➤ Step 17: Mistakes Are Good; Step 24: What If?; Step 35: Changing Behaviour; Step 36: Moving On

8 Overcoming Barriers

The more we discover about how the mind works, the more we realize that thinking and feeling are intimately intertwined. Whether you are picking a new item of clothing or deciding which person to appoint at an interview, emotions play a huge part in your decision-making process. For perception is selective. If you are feeling angry, then small, inconsequential things can irritate you. If you are afraid, then an otherwise nondescript noise may frighten you. If you are feeling very happy, then silly events can bring a smile to your face.

"A fact is like a sack – it won't stand up if it's empty. To make it stand up, first you have to put in it all the reasons and feelings that caused it in the first place."

LUIGI PIRANDELLO (1867–1936)

Negative emotions threaten your ability to learn; they can cause you to lose confidence or concentration, make it hard to cope with complex issues and make you feel unable to keep going when things get tough.

Most common emotional barriers can be divided into cultural, structural and personal issues. Cultural barriers involve factors such as peer pressure, alienation, lack of experience, or attitudes to gender or age. Structural barriers are caused by constraints such as a lack of time or money. Personal barriers involve negative feelings and associations such as a lack of self-belief or low motivation.

EXERCISE: Troubleshooting

Think of yourself as if you were a computer that has temporarily gone wrong. Imagine you are turning to the section on troubleshooting that you find in most manuals. Use a chart such as the one below to tackle your own problems. Identifying the emotional causes of a problem will help you to move on to find practical solutions.

Problem	Causes	Solutions
I feel nervous when speaking in public	Lack of practice Fear of failure	Try calming exercises (see page 29) Watch others and practise
I'm no good at learning	Low self-esteem Bad past experiences/ associations with learning	Try different methods Break things up into manageable chunks (see Step 19)
I keep getting stuck	Pessimistic mindset Lack of experience	Work on developing optimism (see Step 7) and persistence (see Step 13)
I always lose arguments	Lack of confidence Not thinking through approach carefully enough	Try developing your negotiation skills (see Steps 40, 44, 45 and 47)
I haven't got enough time	Busy lifestyle Lots of commitments	Prioritize Make and keep to a schedule

9 Adjusting Attitudes

In this chapter we have been exploring the importance of mindset. In particular we have looked at ways of developing a positive, optimistic approach to learning, and ways of overcoming emotional barriers to your development. But what about those attitudes that are likely to impede your development?

There are a number of bad attitudes that can prevent you from using your mind most effectively and creatively, and which are likely to cause distress to those around you, too. Some of the most common include disowning: pretending that you are not responsible for the way you behave; blaming: finding fault in others rather than in yourself; and criticizing: being too quick to tell other people where their thinking falls short.

These habits will alienate others, and cause an atmosphere of resentment. Rather, you need to nurture positive habits in yourself to create a climate of cooperation and support, which is conducive to boosting the performance of your mind. This is easy to say, but not always so easy to do!

However, it is possible. Your temperament is not set in stone. The habits you have learned can be unlearned. If you choose to, you can identify your negative habits and work on building up your mental muscles so that you are strong enough to change some of them.

EXERCISE: Develop Helpful Habits

This exercise is designed to help you kick-start the process of developing helpful habits and identifying and changing less helpful ones.

1. In a notebook, draw a chart with two columns: one for Good Habits and the other for Bad Habits. In your first column, make a list of those habits which you currently possess and want to develop further because they are positive and in the second column those which you want to change because they are not.
2. You might then like to use a second chart to think about how to encourage your positive habits and put an end to negative ones. For example, if you think you have an inquisitive nature, you might want to practise asking leading questions to stretch your mind. If you are quick to criticize others, you might decide to work on developing empathy or rethink your approach to giving and receiving feedback.
3. Remember to focus on the positive first. And if there is more than one item on your Bad Habits list, just try working on one of them to begin with!

➤➤ Step 20: How to Ask Good Questions; Step 35: Changing Behaviour; Step 41: Giving and Receiving Feedback; Step 43: Walking in Other People's Shoes

10 Worst-case Scenarios

Sometimes when something bad or disappointing happens to you it can seem like the beginning of the end. In such situations it helps to remember two things: first, if you are going to boost your mind you are bound to make mistakes; and second, events are often not as bad as they first appear to be.

It was Russian psychologist Lev Vygotsky who, in the 1920s and 1930s, first described the simple but powerful idea of the Zone of Proximal Development. This zone bridges the gap between what is known and what can be known. People who exercise their minds are always trying to move on from the comfort zone to the grow zone. As this is always more challenging than remaining in the comfort zone, mistakes are bound to be made. Indeed, making mistakes and learning from them is an essential component of mental growth.

Of course, things can go wrong whether or not you are consciously trying to tackle something difficult. At such times your mindset will be very important. If you can achieve a sense of perspective that ensures you can be positive while recognizing that you are facing a difficult situation, so much the better.

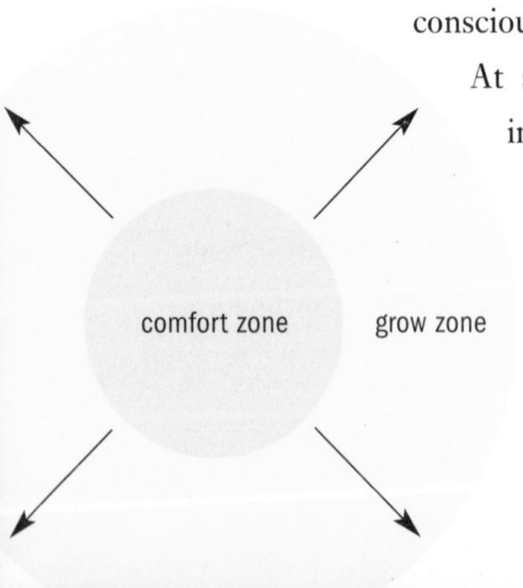

comfort zone

grow zone

EXERCISE: It Can't Be That Bad

This exercise draws on approaches which are used in cognitive therapy and in neuro-linguistic programming. There are two elements to it: first, putting the issue in perspective and then seeing it from other points of view.

1 Think of something that is making you unhappy at present or, if you prefer, practise using a potential problem or an imaginary scenario.
2 Clearly state what your particular problem is.
3 However severe your problem may seem, see if you can imagine how it could be even worse. If you are grieving the loss of a relationship, think how much worse it could be if you had also just lost your job, become seriously ill or didn't have a friend or family member to confide in. Really stretch your mind. However painful or difficult this may be, when you return to your actual situation, you may find it easier to see it in context.
4 Try and see things from two other viewpoints: first, from the perspective of someone else who is affected by the situation, and second, from the viewpoint of an imaginary bystander. Push yourself to imagine what they might see in the the situation that isn't wholly awful!
5 Reflect on the fruits of your imagining and see if the problem is not quite as bad as you first thought.

➤➤Step 7: Being Half Full; Step 17: Mistakes Are Good; Step 36: Moving On

11 Ready, Go, Steady

This is a model that I have developed, which looks at learning as a three-stage process, although there are overlaps between the stages.

Ready

Before you embark on improving your mind power, you need to be emotionally ready. This involves feeling confident and good about yourself (see Steps 7 and 8). But it is more than this. Think of a time when you have started on something but given up on it within weeks. Maybe the effort involved was greater than you had imagined? Perhaps you were disheartened because you felt that you had failed? The decision to give up is usually rooted in a lack of motivation and a common cause of lost motivation is fear of failure.

A good example of this is learning to drive a car. If you have failed your driving test several times, then you may feel disinclined to get back in a car and practise some more. Here it is essential to imagine the bigger picture – hold in mind the pleasure you will feel when you do pass and the new opportunities it will open up.

Part of the skill of using your mind effectively is an ability to read your own moods. Recognize you are stressed, angry or defensive, and you can work on dealing with these negative emotions first, so that when you start something new you are in the right state of mind.

Go

The next stage is to have at your fingertips a range of strategies that work for you. We all learn in different ways, and different tasks also require different methods.

You have already learned about some of your preferences. Were you able to identify yourself in Step 1 with particular types of intelligence? If so, then you can use this to help you develop successful strategies. If you tend to visualize things, say, you might find it most helpful to draw diagrams and use images to enhance your learning. The learning styles explored in Step 2 will have also helped you to build a clearer picture of yourself, how you absorb information, approach new things and make decisions.

Take a moment to look back to the Honey and Mumford categories (pages 18–19). Which described you best? When tackling something that you know you find difficult, choose a method that you feel comfortable with.

an Activist tends toward:	a Pragmatist tends toward:
Games • Role-play	Informal learning • Networking
Job swaps • Trial and Error	On the job learning • Searching the Web
a Reflector tends toward:	**a Theorist tends toward:**
Coaching • Keeping a diary	Instruction • Lecture
Peer review • Questioning	Reading • Study guides and manuals

Let's suppose you are thinking about getting a new job and want to brush up on your interview skills. An Activist might enlist the help of a friend to role-play interviewer and interviewee, so that they can practise both asking and answering tough questions. A Theorist might prefer to read up and make notes on different interview styles.

Steady

How often have you thought to yourself that you are too busy to take stock and learn the lessons of a particular event? A deadline is looming; you have to go and pick up the children; you've got an urgent appointment. There always seem to be endless pressing reasons for not taking time to reflect. Yet in some ways, this is the most important part of the mind-boosting process. The challenge for us all is to harvest the lessons of our life as we hurtle through it.

People who use their minds really effectively allow themselves time to reflect on what they have done: how they did it, what worked well and is worth using again, where the mistakes occurred, what the experience has taught them, and so on.

To prompt your mind into searching out this sort of analysis, try routinely asking yourself questions such as "What went well?" or "Where could I have done better?" and building in a few minutes at the start of each meeting, each project, each family day out, to recall what you have learned since the last time.

CHECKLIST: How to Use the Ready, Go, Steady Approach

Try this approach to whatever you have to face in the near future. It might be something at home (how to be more patient with your children), at work (how to chair effective meetings) or for yourself (learning to draw).

Ready:
Get yourself emotionally prepared and motivated. Have a plan to encourage you should your motivation falter.

➤➤ Step 1: Different Kinds of Smart; Step 2: Your Learning Style; Step 7: Being Half Full; Step 8: Overcoming Barriers; Step 13: Keeping Going

Go:
Choose which method or methods are best suited to you and to the task.

➤➤ Chapter 4: Useful Techniques; Step 29: Making It Stick; Step 39: Listening Carefully

Steady:
Take stock of your progress. Consider whether you need help, and what kind.

➤➤ Step 16: Taking Stock; Step 17: Mistakes Are Good; Step 41: Giving and Receiving Feedback

CHAPTER 3

Helpful Habits

You may genuinely want to boost your mind power, and by now you will have an idea of how your mind works, which learning styles suit you and the kind of mindset that you need to adopt, but unless you are prepared to become more aware of the practical habits which are likely to be most helpful, your dream may remain just that – a dream.

Perhaps there is some truth about learning in the words of American writer Mark Twain: "Do something every day that you don't want to do. This is the golden rule for acquiring the habit of doing your duty without pain." Certainly, whether it is your duty or not, if it is your choice to become more effective, then you may have to consciously try things out and practise them until they become more instinctive.

In this chapter you will learn about some essential habits to acquire: how to concentrate, how to become more persistent, how to slow down when necessary, why reflection and mistakes are important and how it is sometimes smart to bide your time and be patient.

12 Concentration

Along with a relaxed yet alert state of mind and good motivation, an ability to concentrate is vital to boosting your mental capacity. Our minds are, according to British learning guru Guy Claxton, "wayward": they have minds of their own! So interested are they in what is going on and so good at making connections – often drawing on our deepest and most unconscious thoughts – that it can be difficult to make them prioritize what we want them to do.

There are two stages to concentrating. First, you need to banish distraction and clutter. This involves discipline and time management. Most people feel more calm and alert early in the day. If this is true of you, use this time for tackling "brain jobs". It's all too easy to be distracted by the thought of a second cup of coffee, so tell yourself before you start that you'll break in, say, 30 minutes. Get into the routine of performing less stimulating tasks, such as making perfunctory phone calls, at other times. This discipline will help you use your most productive period more effectively.

Second, you need to centre your attention. Research has shown that when you pay attention to something the parts of the brain that process information become more active. It's as if you are wearing a special head-torch which illuminates specifically what you want to see rather than everything around you.

TECHNIQUE 1: Clear Your Mind

Practise the following techniques, to help you clear your mind and concentrate on the priority of the moment.

- Be ruthless about setting aside time and space. Find somewhere quiet and comfortable, turn off your phone and tell the family you need quiet time.
- Close your eyes and take a few deep breaths. Let your mind go blank.
- If there are irritating, distracting ideas burdening your mind, try jotting them down, then consciously forget about them. Often this will free up your mind.

TECHNIQUE 2: Pay Attention

It's easy to read a page of a book and realize that your mind has wandered off. Try these devices to help you remain actively engaged:

- Highlight words or sentences which seem important and compile a list of any questions as you go along.
- If you are trying to commit something to memory, stop every 10 minutes and see if you can jot down what you have learned so far.
- Summarize the data visually – make a thumbnail sketch or draw a diagram.

➤➤ Step 6: Relaxed Alertness; Step 8: Overcoming Barriers; Step 13: Keeping Going; Step 25: Mind Mapping®

13 Keeping Going

We have all heard of the saying, "practice makes perfect." Perhaps you can still hear the voice of a teacher who was always nagging you to work harder? Or maybe it was one of your parents in their keenness for you to do well? Quite possibly you were irritated by their advice – most of us are at some stage in our lives! But if you want to boost your mind power, then learning how to stick with something – or developing persistence – is an essential skill.

The 10 year rule

After many years of research, Swedish Dr K. Anders Ericsson has proposed what he calls the 10 year rule. This states that the highest levels of performance seem to require about 10 years' intense practice. Most interestingly, he suggests that almost anyone can become exceptionally good at something if they are prepared to put in the necessary time.

There are three main areas that you will need to work on if you want to be able to stick with things: understanding yourself, knowing how to deal with difficulties and being able to tolerate uncertainty. Here we will explore the first two areas and we will cover the third section – tolerating uncertainty – in Chapter 6, which focuses on dealing with change.

Understanding yourself

You need to focus on what motivates you to learn. We all have different drivers. Curiosity, the dream of a new job, a better quality of life, improved self-confidence, a desire to stretch your brain – all of these are possible drivers of motivation. But they are also relatively abstract concepts. For most people the reality of motivation has more to do with practical factors.

What can you do to enhance your confidence if you are feeling low? Talk to a friend? What kind of rewards can you give yourself as you make progress? Some special "me" time? How do you deal with the many distractions which will inevitably present themselves? Allocate a specific time slot for uninterrupted "brain work"? Of course, the ways in which you keep yourself motivated are personal and you will need to choose the methods that work best for you.

"Genius is one percent inspiration and 99 percent perspiration."
THOMAS EDISON (1847–1931)

It is useful to remember that our brains work in a very similar way to our bodies. If you want to get your body fit, you might go to a gym and work out. After five minutes or so of hard exercise, you will start to feel the strain, but as you keep going, you will gradually begin to get fitter. Similarly, the more you exercise your learning muscles and keep going when things feel tough, the fitter your brain will become.

Knowing how to deal with difficulties

Most people would agree that anything that is worth doing in life will have its difficult moments. This is certainly true of improving your mind; it's so easy to give up when you get stuck. But effective people develop ways of dealing with the challenges they face.

When you are faced with a difficulty it's a good idea to play to your strengths and use your preferred learning style(s). However, sometimes a task can appear so huge and intimidating that we don't know where to begin. The simplest and most effective way of tackling large, complex challenges is to break them down into more easily digestible bite-sized chunks. Working on and completing small, manageable tasks will encourage you to give 100 percent effort to every little thing you do, which will, in turn, inspire you to keep going – bringing you closer to your overall goal and increasing your likelihood of success.

Two of the most common difficulties that you are likely to experience are mental blocks and a lack of stamina. The technique opposite will help you learn how to identify and overcome these specific barriers to persistence.

➤➤ Step 7: Being Half Full; Step 8: Overcoming Barriers; Step 12: Concentration; Step 19: Big and Small Pictures; Step 22: Visualization; Step 51: Setting Goals

TECHNIQUE: Staying Power

When you find yourself wanting to give up, try to identify the reason.

- Is it emotional? Anxiety making you reluctant to start writing a speech? Boredom on a study course?
- Is it practical? Computer acting up? A cancelled course?
- Is it a person? An officious official? A persistently awkward colleague?
- Is it physical? Too tired to concentrate so that you keep having to start again? Recurring backache causing you discomfort?

Take a little time on this. A "disobedient" computer may make you angry, but if the real problem is practical, it requires a practical solution in which emotions play no part! Once you have found the reason, try one or more of the following:

1. If you have been stuck like this before, think back to what you did then. See if it works now.
2. List all the things you could do, and choose one you have not tried before.
3. Seek advice. Ring up a friend and talk it through. Or call in a professional, whether it's a chiropractor or a computer whiz who's needed. Or surf the Internet for help.
4. Try some visualization. Picture how great you will feel after successfully completing whatever it is.
5. Tackle fatigue. Do some energetic stretching, or have a week of early nights.

14 Soft Focus

One of the problems with our minds is that they are just too efficient! Hardly have we given them something to gnaw away at and they have found the solution. Or have they? Often, all our minds have done is come up with something obvious and familiar – a superficial response to a complex problem. With a little less haste they might have thought of something more original and effective.

Difficult issues are not about to give up their answers in a trice. Sometimes it takes time for a pattern to emerge from a series of clues. And it helps if you can put your brain into soft focus mode.

Think of those optical illusion pictures where you are confronted with a series of shapes and asked what you can see. The more you look for the answer the less likely you are to see it. Whereas, when you stop straining at the leash and try looking through "slow eyes", then an apparently random arrangement of meaningless splodges becomes, say, the intricate markings of a butterfly's wing.

If you are always in a hurry, your brain will probably take the easy way out. But if you can get into the habit of giving yourself time to ponder, then it may well come up with something really interesting, creative and different – something out of its normal groove.

➤➤Step 21: Finding the Problem; Step 24: What If?

EXERCISE: **Looking Through Slow Eyes**

Look at these pictures. What do you see?

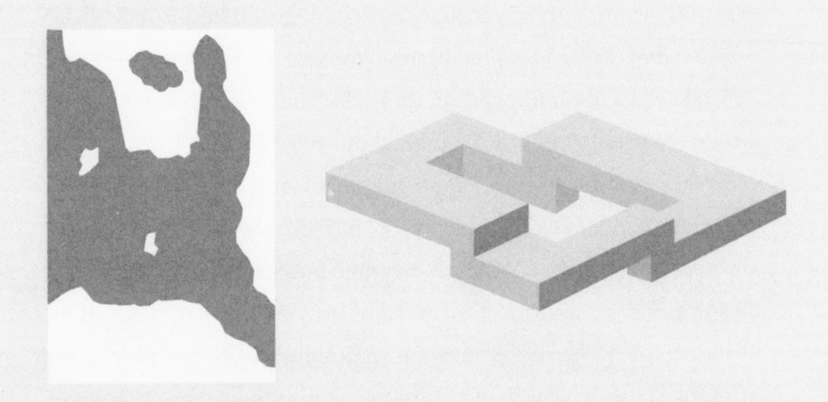

Can you see a bearded man in the first picture? Try looking at it with slow eyes. Let your eyes go almost out of focus and just wait and see if the patterns begin to resolve themselves into a shape. Now can you see a face?*

Are the steps leading up or down in the second picture? Try to climb them in your mind's eye. Which is the bottom step and which is the top?

Whenever you are faced with a puzzle or a challenge, try slowing down and waiting to see if your brain can make sense of the clues it is getting.

*His left eye is visible, his right eye is in shadow. The beard hides the lower part of the face.

15 Pause for Thought

When feelings become too intense, they can get in the way of you using your mind. For many people this can happen all too easily when they are under stress, very tired or finding a particular relationship difficult. The better you get at reading your own tell-tale signs of an impending difficulty, the more likely you are to be able to avoid emotions clouding your mind.

American management expert Stephen Covey has suggested that we all have a "pause button" which, just like the switch on a DVD or video player, freezes the action when you press it. So, if you are heading for an argument with your boss or partner, you might decide to press the pause button to gain some breathing space to see if there is a smarter way of continuing. This might take the form of saying something like: "It feels like we are approaching this from different points of view. Let me sleep on it and talk to you again in the morning." Or "We're both tired and hungry, let's take a break and talk again after supper."

The pause button idea can also work well if you are doing some intense learning. When things get really tough and you find yourself stuck or unable to concentrate, you can press the pause button. Take some time out – go for a walk around the block – and return to your task with a new release of energy.

TECHNIQUE: Using Your Pause Button

Buying yourself a bit of emotional thinking time is a really useful strategy at home and at work. It is definitely something that is much easier to use for real if you have practised it beforehand.

1 Start by taking a member of your family or a colleague into your confidence and explaining the pause button idea to them. Think of some shared moments in the past when emotions have run high and pressing the pause button might have been a good idea.
2 Agree to start using the pause button idea. This will involve having some simple signals or trigger words which can be used in the heat of the moment to suggest that you freeze the emotional action and take time out.
3 Give people positive feedback when they have tried using or responding to this technique. Discuss what worked well and what worked less well. Is there anything you could do to make it work more successfully next time? For example, you might want to try pressing the pause button earlier, or taking more time out before you resume.

You will probably find that the pause button is a useful way of avoiding unnecessarily negative situations which can so easily sap your mental energy.

➤➤Step 40: How to Disagree; Step 41: Giving and Receiving Feedback; Step 47: Dealing with Conflict

16 Taking Stock

Do you ever wonder why you keep making the same mistakes? Or why things always seem to go wrong for you in certain situations? If so, you may be in need of some time to reflect on what you have learned. For, if you can't reflect on events and take stock, then you will find it hard to improve.

In a sense, reflection is the key to extracting meaning from your life. You could use the equation: Living + Reflection = Learning. Your mind makes connections between things and then constructs patterns. This ability harks back to primitive times when it was essential to our ancestors' survival. They would see a lion eating its prey, make the connection that lions might be threatening creatures and file the lion in the category "dangerous animals".

So efficient is your mind that it has often done its reflection without you being aware of it. And so, although we are learning all the time, we sometimes find it difficult to be sure of what we have learned and how we did so. You may know intuitively that you managed a certain task or situation well, but unless you can describe what has happened in more detail you will not be able to share what you have learned with others or consolidate your learning in your own mind so that you can draw on this knowledge in the future. Your goal needs to be to make conscious reflection a way of being.

EXERCISE: A Learning Log

A learning log is a simple method of recording what happens to you, the conclusions you draw and what you might do differently as a result. It's a kind of diary with three columns running through it.

What happened and when	My key learning points	What I would like to do differently

1. Reproduce this chart over some pages in a notebook. Then think back over a recent experience. What happened? Try focusing on a small part of it. Write out a description of what happened without yet thinking about what you learned.
2. Now explore what happened. What were the key learning points?
3. With every learning experience there are usually some aspects that you could improve on. Plan what you are going to do differently next time you encounter a similar situation. Try to write down how you are going to do it.

Try to keep a learning log for a week. If you find it helpful, you could do it more often and for longer periods of time or even on a continual basis.

➤➤ Step 11: Ready, Go, Steady; Step 17: Mistakes Are Good; Step 27: Know-how and Knowledge Transfer

17 Mistakes Are Good

Far too many people see mistakes as a sign of failure. And in an increasingly competitive and litigious society, failure has huge amounts of opprobrium attached to it. But if you really want to develop your mind, then you need to start seeing mistakes as something to learn from rather than something to be ashamed about. For mistakes are the raw material of learning.

As we have seen, to respond to mistakes effectively you need to be able to notice them, reflect on them, and then adapt what you do next time accordingly. If you can do this on a regular basis, then your mistakes begin to have a real value to you.

> *"Experience is the name we give to our mistakes."*
> OSCAR WILDE (1854-1900)

Indeed, for creativity to flourish, you need to take risks and try lots of things out in the knowledge that only some of them will work. And if you are deliberately doing things outside of your comfort zone, you are bound to fail sometimes. So, if failure is an inevitable part of challenging yourself, then to sometimes fail becomes a smart thing to do – provided that you learn from failure and resolve to do things differently next time around.

➤➤Step 10: Worst-case Scenarios; Step 16: Taking Stock; Step 27: Know-how and Knowledge Transfer; Step 41: Giving and Receiving Feedback

TECHNIQUE 1: Learn from Your Mistakes

Next time you make a mistake, try my **LEARN** approach:

Listen to what people around you have to say. Try not to be defensive and, instead, see yourself as others see you.

Evaluate what happened. Why did things go wrong? What could you have done differently? See chart on page 57.

Acknowledge your mistake. Having the courage to admit your mistakes is a sign of strength.

Remember what you did. If you make a conscious effort to remember your mistake, you will be less likely to repeat it.

Never blame others. Instead, try and work out how you will act next time.

TECHNIQUE 2: Learn from Your Successes

You don't only learn from your mistakes, you can learn from your successes, too. So get into the habit of recognizing good experiences, such as a child's bedtime that went unusually smoothly or a potentially tricky negotiation that turned out well for you. Also try writing down one thing at the end of each day that has been important to you and why. Ask friends, family and colleagues to help you by giving you regular feedback. This will encourage you to identify common factors of good experiences, and alert you to any patterns of bad ones.

18 Deferring Judgment

Have you come across the fable of four blind men and an elephant? One man believes the leg he is grasping to be a tree. The second man is sure that the tusk he is holding is a spear. A third is convinced that the writhing trunk he is touching is a snake. The last, feeling an ear, tells his companions that he has found a fan. If only the men had waited a bit and pooled their knowledge, they might have been able to make sufficient connections to realize that they were, in fact, dealing with an elephant.

Being able to defer your judgment, not jump to conclusions, is a useful attribute to have if you wish to improve your mind. In today's judgmental society it often seems as if you need to have a smart answer to everything. Not being able to come up with an immediate sound-bite response can be perceived as a weakness. Yet this quality of delayed judgment is exactly what many complex situations require. It allows you to move beyond simplistic notions into more sophisticated ones.

Tough problems take time to unpack. If you are too eager to solve them and strain away at the leash desperately trying to come up with an answer, your mind becomes brittle and binary. It can't see beyond the black and white, the yesses and nos.

Many of the problems you face are ambiguous and possibly even contradictory. For example, if something is smouldering, do you blow on it if you want to put it out? Yes if it is a match. No if it is an ember in a fire. To come up with an effective solution you must wait and evaluate the individual circumstances.

Take a moment to think about some of the issues being raised here. Can you think of situations when you may have benefited from putting your judgment on hold? Perhaps there have been times when you've been listening to other people's ideas, and you jumped too quickly into a conversation? Or when you dismissed someone else's idea too hastily?

Maybe there have been times when you have felt confused and quickly came up with an answer, but would have benefited from spending more time puzzling out a *better* answer? Or when you have been exploring a really difficult problem which may have had many different perspectives? Have there been times when you dismissed something as unimportant which subsequently assumed much greater significance in your life? Or when things have been difficult and you made an emotional judgment that you later regretted? By becoming aware of these situations you can consciously practise deferring your judgment the next time you are in a similar situation, and with time and practice this response will become instinctive.

Deferring judgment is an important part of what it is to be creative, and is especially instrumental to generating ideas. This is something we have to do, whether sitting around the kitchen table working out where the family will go on holiday this year, wondering how to deal with a leaking pipe in the middle of the night or in a brainstorming session at work. More often than not, such situations involve a spirit of collaboration.

It is smart to defer evaluation when working with others to come up with new ideas, for three good reasons. First, if you jump in too quickly, especially with a critical thought, you are likely to make the contributor of the idea feel put down. This can evoke hostility or cause the person to withdraw from the discussion.

Second, coming up with creative ideas is a dynamic, ongoing process. Ideas breed ideas. Often the better ideas come later as a result of earlier ones. By postponing judgment, you will enable yourself and others to go through this creative process. And third, if you are serious about developing your mind, then you may want to work on the personality which comes with it. People who never stop and think are hard work to be with!

➤➤ Step 14: Soft Focus; Step 21: Finding the Problem; Step 23: Using Your Intuition; Step 24: What If?; Step 43: Walking in Other People's Shoes

EXERCISE: **Playing a Waiting Game**

You can get better at delaying your judgment when it is needed by practising with imaginary complex situations.

Imagine being asked each of the following questions. What is your first reaction? What is your considered opinion? Is there a difference between the two?

1. What three wishes would you most like granted?
2. Who are the three most important people in your life?
3. What is the one place on Earth which you would find most exciting to be spirited off to?
4. What do you believe in so strongly that you would be willing to die for it?
5. If you could have whatever job you wanted, what would it be and why?
6. If you were the most powerful person in the world, what could you do to end all violence?

Which areas of your life currently present you with issues which require a large measure of your judgment? Are there any patterns to them? Is it to do with people or environments or situations or something else?

CHAPTER 4

Useful Techniques

In this chapter you will learn some techniques which will prove invaluable in helping you to boost your mind power. They will not turn you into a genius overnight, but if you work to acquire these skills and practise applying them to different situations, then you will undoubtedly grow in confidence and effectiveness.

The danger with our minds is that they too often rely on what they have done before. So, if your repertoire is narrow, you will rapidly run out of steam. In this chapter you will have the chance to expand your range and become more resourceful. You will learn how to break complex tasks down into their component parts; and practise asking good questions, getting to the root of the problem, clarifying issues, thinking intuitively and using the knowledge you have gained in different parts of your life. And you can learn techniques which may be new to you such as visualization and Mind Mapping®.

19 Big and Small Pictures

Have you ever tried to do a jigsaw puzzle without referring to the picture on the lid of the box? Without knowing where the bulk of the sky is or if an expanse of a certain green is grass or a hedge, it can be very difficult to make sense of all the little blue and green pieces. You need to concentrate on the detail of each piece but at the same time try to envisage the whole picture.

Much of thinking and learning is like this: seeing the wood as well as being able to pick out the individual trees. Smart minds see both the big picture and the little pictures which make up the whole.

Often it helps to start with the big picture and break it down into smaller chunks. This way you can be more confident that your efforts are not going to be wasted. Each of the smaller chunks become achievements in their own right as well as the building-blocks of your larger project, and you gain an increasing sense of satisfaction as you work your way through them.

"Chunking" – a useful technique

When breaking up larger issues or activities into smaller, more manageable elements, you need to be clear of your goal – sometimes chunks can be aspects of a bigger subject; sometimes they are the component parts of a process.

Let's imagine you want to refurbish your bathroom. The kind of chunks that would help you to address different *aspects* of its design and decoration might include:

- working out a budget
- planning the layout
- investigating sanitaryware
- checking plumbing regulations
- experimenting with colour
- choosing light fixtures
- trying out tiling effects
- considering forms of heating

Whereas the *process* of decorating your bathroom might break down into chunks that include:

- stripping
- plumbing
- plastering
- tiling
- painting
- finishing touches

Of course, each of these areas can be broken down into even smaller chunks, so that tiling could include cutting tiles, using tile cement, grouting, and so on.

Breaking down a complicated process or a large project into chunks like this not only makes it more manageable but also helps you do it more efficiently – in considering what's involved in achieving your new bathroom you can also plan the best order to do each step and avoid, say, the plumber turning up before the bath.

Getting the big picture

While reducing a large project into chunks is definitely helpful, over-concentration on individual pieces can cause you to lose sight of the big picture. For example, you might become so involved in planning the route and timetable for a sailing holiday that you quite overlook the fact that your youngest child gets chronically seasick!

Grasping the big picture can also help when you find yourself in the middle of something you do not quite understand. This can be true for anything from writing a report to preparing and cooking a complicated meal. A typical example of this at work is arriving a little late at a meeting and finding that you do not have the faintest idea what is going on! Either there is no agenda, or if there is it does not seem to provide the overall plan of the meeting's aims. People are throwing in ideas or comments at random, like (to pick up the analogy I started with) so many pieces of a jigsaw lying on a table in no apparent order. What is lacking is the picture on the box.

In cases such as this, the most helpful thing you can do is to ask questions that will enable you to get enough of the big picture to put the details into context. You might try saying: "Excuse me but I have mislaid my agenda, could someone share theirs?", "Many apologies for being late; could someone possibly just recap on where we are going?" or "I am really finding this difficult to follow. Can we take a moment just to agree what the bigger picture is here?"

EXERCISE: Seeing the Wood *and* the Trees

Think of something that you are trying to tackle or about to embark on. Choose something that is neither too small (such as getting home at 4pm on a Friday) nor too big (as in creating an ideal work-life balance.)

Practise breaking down your chosen area into bite-sized chunks while at the same time maintaining a clear view of the bigger picture. Try one or both of these approaches:

1 Write a word that describes your overall aim at the top of a sheet of paper and then compile a list of all it involves. You might approach this chronologically, and write out all the "ingredients" and methods in the order that they need to be done, like a recipe. Or write each element on a small card or sticky note, so that you can physically move them all around. As you do this, further or smaller chunks may occur to you and you can group some of them together around emerging themes.

2 Use a Mind Map® to help you to visualize the various aspects of your plan. As with the previous suggestion, start with a word or phrase, but this time put it in the middle of your paper and allow your ideas to develop out from it like the branches and roots of a tree.

➤➤Step 20: How to Ask Good Questions; Step 25: Mind Mapping®; Step 26: Clarifying

20 How to Ask Good Questions

When a character in Douglas Adams's *The Hitchhiker's Guide to the Galaxy* says that "the answer to the meaning of life, the universe and everything is 42," we are reminded of the difficulty of answering complex questions. Of course 42 seems like a silly answer. But maybe "What is the meaning of life?" is too big a question for most brains to grapple with.

"Judge a man by his questions rather than by his answers."

VOLTAIRE (1694–1778)

Asking good questions is an important skill. Sometimes a certain problem that confronts you is actually a symptom of another problem. Asking the right questions can help you to identify the core issue. A probing question is a good indicator of your curiosity level, which you need to have set on high to get the best out of your mind.

The most common kinds of questions are those of a factual nature. Often they start with Who, What, Where or When – for example, What is the capital of Denmark? Usually questions like these require an item of information or yes/no answers. But the more interesting questions involve interpretation and judgment. They tend to start with Why or How, and are often open-ended. Asking these kinds of questions encourages you to approach issues from a variety of angles, thus stretching your mind.

TECHNIQUE: Making How? and Why? Work for You

Try these approaches to help you develop good questioning skills.

- Every day, try to think of a why/how question that you do not know the answer to. Make a list of these questions and once a week, or once a fortnight, make time to chat about them with a friend or family member.
- Next time someone says something to you which you do not understand, rather than nodding or pretending that you know what they are talking about, ask them to explain.
- If you are in a meeting or taking part in a discussion and are not sure of its purpose, be brave and ask people to make their aims clear. Phrase your question the right way and you will appear alert and analytical. Try saying, "Excuse me, but I am not sure what we are trying to achieve here; can you clarify this for me?"
- Make a question more specific by turning it into a multiple question. So, "Do you think women are better drivers?" could become, "Would you say that women are a) safer, b) slower, c) more cautious drivers than men?"
- Every time you hear someone asking a good question, whether on the television, on the radio, or in your daily encounters, make a note of it. Later, dissect it and try to discover what makes it work so well.

➤➤ Step 21: Finding the Problem; Step 24: What If?; Step 26: Clarifying

21 Finding the Problem

A problem is a difficult situation that needs to be resolved. We all have to face many of these throughout our life. And smart people are good at defining what the problem is and then coming up with solutions for it.

As mentioned in the previous step, often what appears to be a problem is not the real problem – it's a symptom of another problem. To take a simple example: persistently arriving late for work may be the symptom of an underlying, root problem. The real issue may be one of the following:

- You are going to bed too late and you are too tired to get up on time in the morning
- You leave home too late
- Your method of transport is unreliable
- You need to organize your child care duties differently.

If you can identify the real problem in any situation, then you will avoid wasting time fretting about the wrong thing and you will be better equipped to find a successful solution.

➤➤Step 16: Taking Stock; Step 20: How to Ask Good Questions; Step 26: Clarifying; Step 35: Changing Behaviour

EXERCISE: Getting to the Root of the Matter

Try working your way through these 10 questions for a current problem you have.

1. Who says it is a problem? Is it just you, or do other people agree?
2. How many people are affected?
3. How severe is the problem? If it's just a vague sense of unease, maybe it's not a problem at all.
4. Is it an isolated incident or part of a pattern? Is it persistent?
5. Is it caused by something else? As illustrated by the late for work example opposite, what we at first perceive to be the problem can actually be only a symptom. Think hard about the root cause.
6. Is there just one cause or a number of causes? Are they interdependent or could you tackle each separately?
7. If the problem is caused by others, who are the main protagonists?
8. Is it caused by a situation beyond people's control? If so, what is this?
9. With a persistent problem, what is causing it to remain or recur?
10. What might help to alleviate the trouble or break the cycle?

These are short questions, but they may require a lot of thought to answer fully. It might help to draw a diagram of the problem, who it affects and its ramifications; or else try to condense the real problem into a sentence.

Clarify the situation, ask the right questions and you will find it easier to start thinking of solutions. Actually your amazing brain may have already started!

22 Visualization

It is sometimes said that scenery is much better on the radio. In other words, the power of your imagination can create a more vivid backdrop than film or television. This principle holds when it comes to developing your mind.

Visualization can work in a number of ways. You can use it to remember a sequence of events by closing your eyes and "walking" through it in your mind – for example, mentally re-enacting leaving your keys somewhere or playing winning moves in chess.

You can also use visualization to break or lighten a mood of despondency. In your private visual landscapes you can be anybody and achieve anything. You can picture yourself falling in love with the most beautiful person in the world, running the fastest race, being truly happy. The feelings of elation your visualization brings are real even if the images aren't – just as you really laugh, cry or get excited by a movie. The more you visualize something, the more your brain will begin to imagine that it might just happen. Indeed, athletes use visualization in training. For example, dancers or skiers rehearse their moves in their head as well as in reality. And injured

➤➤ Step 6: Relaxed Alertness; Step 30: Where, When, Why?; Step 48: Good Stress, Bad Stress

athletes have found that even when they cannot physically train, visualizing training and competing can help to improve their eventual performance.

Visualization can also be used as a way of releasing your mind to seek out its own triggers or answers by giving you access to your deeper thoughts and feelings. Pictures can materialize in your brain before you are able to give them names or describe them with words. Images can preserve complexities which words somehow cannot.

EXERCISE: Imagine This...

This exercise is based on one developed with a friend of mine, Professor Guy Claxton. You are going to create an image of somewhere you feel safe, happy and full of energy, somewhere you can go to when seeking answers.

1. First, relax (see page 29). Close your eyes and take three deep breaths.
2. Imagine a beautiful house by a lake. Look out at the lake. What colour is it? What can you see around its edge? Now walk around the house from the outside. What does it look like? Is there a balcony? Where is the front door? Give yourself the key if you need one, and go inside.
3. How many rooms are there? Design each one to suit your different moods. Look out of the windows. Describe the view. Use this imaginary place as your refuge and return to it whenever you want to.

23 Using Your Intuition

In Step 18 we learned that suspending your judgment can help you to answer complex questions and think creatively. I also believe that it can be important sometimes to use your intuition.

Think of the important decisions you have made in your life. For example, making a lifelong commitment to your husband, wife or partner; buying or renting somewhere to live or moving to take a promotion at work. While the decision you made is likely to have involved plenty of rational scrutiny, the chances are that you also had a feeling or hunch that you were doing the right thing – that you just intuitively knew.

Think of the times when you have taken action wholly because something just didn't feel right. A nagging doubt about your relationship with your partner? A concern for the well-being of your child who seemed to be unhappy at the time? An undefinable feeling of dissatisfaction at work? Given that much of what we know exists below the surface of rational thought at an unconscious level, we should not be surprised that this kind of knowing bubbles up from time to time. Smart people know that, just as visualization can help you to become more aware of the subtleties of a situation, so becoming more receptive to your intuition may give you valuable stimuli in approaching a situation or taking a decision.

EXERCISE: Opening Your Mind to Intuitive Responses

This exercise is influenced by work undertaken by American psychologist and author Frances Vaughan. It aims to help you develop your intuitive sense.

1 Think of something that is currently on your mind – a problem or an issue which is not currently being solved through the power of your logical brain.
2 Close your eyes and take yourself back to the dream house that you created in the exercise on page 75.
3 Imagine it is a warm afternoon and you are on the shore of the lake in front of your house. There is a boat nearby and you step into it. You push off gently and lie on your back facing the sky with your eyes closed. You are quite safe and you start to relax. As the evening sets in, you sense it getting dark and drift into a peaceful sleep.
4 When you wake up you have arrived at a beautiful sunlit meadow. All you know is that, in this place, someone will bring you a written message. The message may not seem to solve your problem, but don't worry. Just read it and things will become clearer.
5 Walk back to the boat and return to your dream home. Now reflect on what your message said. See if it offers you any clues. Then open your eyes and return to the present.

➤➤Step 22: Visualization; Step 14: Soft Focus

24 What If?

We all get stuck in ruts, not only in patterns of behaviour, but in ways of thinking, too. Just as it's easy to pick up unhelpful habits of behaviour, it's easy too to fall into predictable ways of thinking. But to improve our minds and come up with fresh perspectives we need to think outside the box. We need to think imaginatively.

Young children find it easy to make-believe, but this ability often escapes us in adulthood. Why is this so? It is not because our brains lose their sparkle. Rather, we are usually so busy that we tend to go for easy, safe options, which normally involve seeing things from the same predictable, often unimaginative, viewpoint.

I believe we all possess the talent of imaginative thinking. We simply need to rediscover this talent and learn how to appropriate it to tackle daily situations. In the 1960s Edward De Bono recognized that to generate new ideas and solutions we need to embrace different perspectives. He described this as "lateral thinking" – the attempt to see all problems as opportunities and create more original and effective ideas. Thinking laterally is particularly useful for grasping new concepts.

►► Step 18: Deferring Judgment; Step 20: How to Ask Good Questions; Step 23: Using Your Intuition

EXERCISE: Thinking Sideways

Try this lateral thinking exercise called Plus, Minus, Interesting, invented by Edward De Bono and widely used throughout the world. It helps you to categorize thoughts and ideas in a way which allows you to consider both sides of an argument. It encourages you to approach issues with an open mind and to come up with creative solutions.

1 Draw three columns in a notebook. Head them: Plus, Minus and Interesting.
2 Choose an idea or proposition. This could be a theoretical, political or environmental issue (for example, road congestion) or a personal dilemma (should your elderly grandmother move to a nursing home?)
3 Explore what is positive (people enjoy owning and driving cars; your grandmother enjoys the company of others). Then what is negative (cars cause delays, accidents, pollution; nursing homes are costly) and what you find interesting about your chosen issue (delays are greater during the school run; your grandmother will be further away, but better cared for).
4 Review your lists. The points you have made under the first two columns can probably be viewed in fixed, polarized terms. However, you should find that the germs of some really good ideas are in the Interesting column (perhaps schools could start earlier and working days could start later, or vice versa; maybe you could plan less frequent but longer visits, combining trips with weekends away).

25 Mind Mapping®

Invented by Tony Buzan in the 1960s, a Mind Map® is a colourful and highly visual way of organizing what is in your mind onto a piece of paper. My example uses Chapter 1 of this book as the

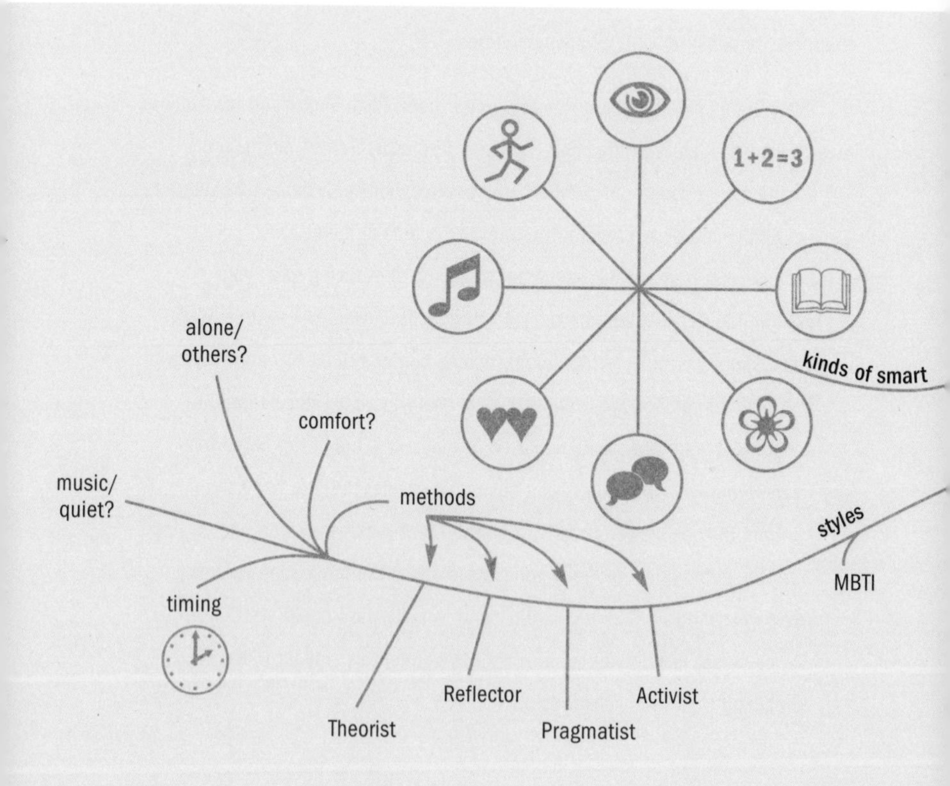

central topic to show its planning at an early stage. The five steps are represented by five main branches. Related themes and topics form sub-branches. When you create a Mind Map® of your own, each main branch should be in a different colour, and you should use images and single words, rather than phrases, wherever possible.

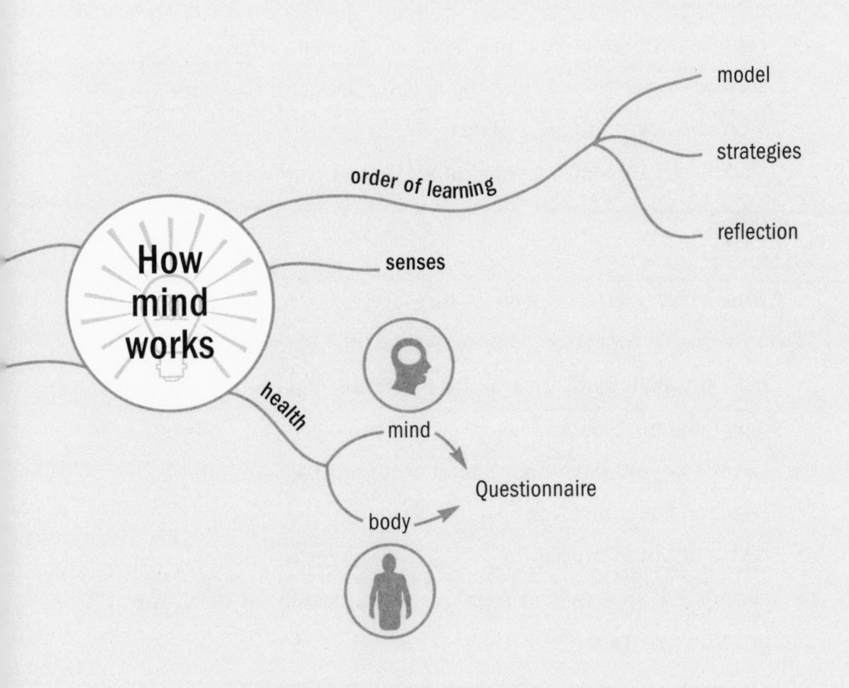

Mind Maps® are an extremely effective learning technique because they encourage you to:

- stop being so linear in your thinking
- escape the boring familiarity of a page of writing
- refrain from counting your ideas into numbered lists
- use colour to make key points more vivid and memorable
- combine graphic images and words for maximum impact
- see how one idea connects to another
- represent the relative importance of different topics
- see the bigger picture and the smaller details at the same time
- view the key points at a glance
- visually fix the data in your mind, so that you remember more
- release your creativity.

Mind Maps® were devised as memory aids, but in fact they are a very versatile tool. You can also use a Mind Map® to:

- help you plan a talk or a written assignment
- generate and clarify ideas about any project
- check that you have understood or memorized something
- take notes in a meeting
- revise for an examination
- summarize an article or topic in a book, lecture or television or radio program.

EXERCISE: Create Your Own Mind Map®

Mind Maps® seem to particularly suit people who find words come to them less naturally than pictures, but they are really useful for anyone wanting to boost their mind power and it is worth investing time learning and practising them. Have a go at creating your own Mind Map® using the guidelines below.

1 Begin with a large sheet of paper and some coloured pens.
2 Choose your subject – this could be any topic that you wish to learn more about, a current project or a personal issue that you need to think about.
3 Start with a key word or picture in the centre of your sheet of paper and work out from this.
4 Draw lines emanating from the centre, like the branches and roots of a tree, for your core thoughts, ideas or themes. Label each main branch with images and/or words (using as few words as possible).
5 Use a different colour for each main branch.
6 Use sub-branches for related ideas.
7 Use arrows or any other visual aids to show links between different strands.
8 Don't get stuck on one branch. If you dry up in one area move on to another.
9 Add organically to your map. Don't judge or hold back.
10 Review your map. Does it capture the key points or issues of your topic? And has creating your map helped to implant these points in your mind?

➤➤ Step 19: Big and Small Pictures; Step 24: What If?

26 Clarifying

In today's complex world it is often difficult to recognize what is important. We are swimming in data, presented with a multitude of problems and faced with difficult and apparently contradictory choices. In organizations, time is wasted every day in meetings where the agenda has not been made clear. In personal relationships, unnecessary unhappiness is caused because people do not say what they mean. And in our written communication, we are often sloppy and ambiguous. How can we best achieve clarity?

It's as simple as A B C D E!

Think of a situation where you have been trying to work something out. Maybe you are toying with the idea of changing your job. Or thinking about moving home. Or wondering why your relationship with your parents is not as good as you would like it to be. Now use my A B C D E approach to help bring clarity to your situation.

A is for Analyze

Start asking yourself some analytical questions about the issue you are exploring, beginning with the big questions. What is the main problem with your current job? While you are dissatisfied with your current home, can you really afford to move? How serious are your concerns about your relationship with your parents? Through analysis you can see if you can tease out the one essential aspect of the situation you are exploring.

B is for Break it down

It is also constructive to break your issue down into smaller chunks, and to look at it from different angles. To help you do this you could sort your sub-issues into two columns labelled with opposites such as good or bad. This will help you to weigh up the possible implications of your issue. However, having only two ways of looking at something often seems like a dilemma. So you may want to add a third category to turn a dilemma into options; for example, "good", "bad" and "something I could live with".

Or you might like to try using a SWOT analysis chart such as the one below. A SWOT chart breaks things down even further, so that you can clearly see what the strengths and weaknesses of your position are and look more closely at the opportunities and threats afforded by aspects of your issue once you have broken it down.

Strengths	Weaknesses
Opportunities	Threats

C is for Criticize your emerging thinking

This is where you need to use why, what, when, how, where and who type approaches. Why do you want to change your job when there are lots of aspects to it that you really enjoy? How will your children cope with having to change schools if you move house? When did you began to feel uncomfortable about your relationship with your parents? The answers to your questions will begin to provide you with a more critical perspective.

D is for Describe what you are thinking

The theorist Graham Wallas once remarked, "How do I know what I think till I see what I say?" Many people find that the act of writing or talking helps to kick-start the process of clarification. It is equally true that if you can accurately describe something to someone else, you are well on the road to understanding it yourself.

E is for Exclude the noise

Finally, make some space for yourself, possibly alone. Go for a walk or do whatever helps to create some uninterrupted thinking time.

Once you have completed this process, it is important to keep some kind of record: a short list of priorities or key words, a set of questions to which you still need answers – whatever works for you.

EXERCISE: How to Achieve Clarity

Practise using the A B C D E approach to help you to explore a complex issue you are currently working on.

Analyze: Get to grips with the situation. Make a note of what the core issue is.

➤➤ Steps 21: Finding the Problem; 24: What If?; 25: Mind Mapping®

Break it down: Divide the issue into more manageable chunks, and try approaching them from different angles. Use the suggestions on page 85.

➤➤ Steps 19: Big and Small Pictures; 24: What If?

Criticize: Nurture your inquisitive nature - ask lots of probing questions and ask other people for their opinion, too.

➤➤ Steps 20: How to Ask Good Questions; 41: Giving and Receiving Feedback

Describe: If you cannot describe the issue in one clear sentence, you probably have not yet achieved clarity, so keep going!

Exclude: Cut out the peripherals. Don't get side-tracked by other related but less central issues.

➤➤ Steps 6: Relaxed Alertness; 12: Concentration

27 Know-how and Knowledge Transfer

There are many different types of knowledge, from facts to opinions, trivial data to great wisdom. But one of the most important types is know-how. Often very difficult to write down, know-how is an understanding of a process, such as how to fix a leak or write concisely or calm someone who is distressed.

If you were to picture your own know-how as one part of your total knowledge, then it would be like the roots of a tree which lie below the earth's surface. In other words, know-how is not always immediately apparent, but it is fundamental to your learning. So it is important to learn the value of know-how and recognize how it can be applied in different circumstances.

Recognizing your know-how

People often overlook a skill or ability because it has become second nature to them: "Surely everyone can do that," they say in surprise. In reality, though, it has been acquired through regular practice and learning. For example, people who can swim can usually only do so after plenty of lessons and practice. Recognizing what you know is a valuable asset and gives you confidence. So:

- acknowledge what you are good at!
- set aside regular time to practise your skills.

Transferring your knowledge

In this example, American psychologists Mary Gick and Keith Holyoak gave college students the following problem:

Imagine you were a doctor faced with a patient who has an inoperable stomach tumour. You have at your disposal rays that can destroy human tissue when directed with sufficient intensity. At lower intensity the rays are harmless to healthy tissue, but they do not affect the tumour either. How can you use these rays to destroy the tumour without destroying the surrounding healthy tissue.

Few students found this problem easy to solve. But nine out of 10 were able to do so when they were also given the following passage:

A general wants to capture a fortress in the centre of a country. There are many roads radiating outward from the fortress. All have been mined so that while groups of men can pass over the roads safely, larger forces will detonate the mines. A full-scale direct attack is therefore impossible. The general's solution is to divide his army into small groups, send each group to the head of a different road and have them converge simultaneously on the fortress.

The students spotted the analogy between dividing the troops up into small groups and using a number of small doses of radiation which converged on the same bit of the tumour. In other words, they were able to transfer a solution for the second problem to the first.

Recognizing know-how enables you to see how skill in one area can help you out in a situation that may seem at first completely unfamiliar. We do this all the time as we transfer from job to job, but knowledge transfer can help in circumstances as wide-ranging as cooking a meal, mending an appliance or mediating in an argument. Transferring know-how knowledge is a complex matter. One very important factor is the extent of your knowledge. You need to know enough about something before you can really use what you know effectively. So, try to achieve an adequate level of knowledge before applying that knowledge elsewhere. For example, you will find it less daunting and tiring to drive a hired car abroad if you are first a confident, competent driver in your own car on home turf.

Context and environment matter. You may be able to use your arguing and persuasion skills very easily with someone you know and love – for example, with your partner or a close friend – but go to pieces when you try to use the same knowledge in front of your overbearing boss.

The examples opposite should help you to identify your know-how and learn how to transfer that knowledge and skill to different parts of your life.

TECHNIQUE: Apply Your Know-how

Use these practical examples to help you get better at using what you know.

- Try to identify processes or elements that are common to different tasks.
  For example:
  If you're learning Spanish, draw on any knowledge you have of Latin or another Latin-based language for their similarities in vocabulary and grammar.
  You may not have organized a big wedding before, but perhaps your skills from organizing another important event, such as planning a dinner party, booking a holiday or setting up a seminar, will be helpful.

- Once you have learned something, apply it in different situations.
  For example:
  A child using a colour-coded table to list different kinds of chemicals in a science class might use a similar table to list dates and events in a history class.
  Learning on a training course how to deal more effectively with other people at work may be adapted to your family life.

Improving Your Memory

As we all live longer and as more and more data flood our daily lives, learning how to remember becomes increasingly important. We find we have to remember passwords, PIN numbers and security codes as well as birthdays, anniversaries and appointments.

But having a good memory extends beyond being able to regurgitate facts and figures on demand. Improving your memory helps your mind work more smartly in almost every area of your life, from increasing your social skills as you unfailingly remember people's names to being able to bring your memories of past experiences to your aid when situations recur. Without the ability to remember there would be no learning, because as soon as you had learned something you would forget it!

Memory is a hugely complex subject and, like an iceberg, most of it exists below the surface of our consciousness. Nevertheless, this chapter includes many useful techniques and approaches which you can learn and apply in your life.

28 The Making of Memories

Much of the time your brain stores and retrieves information without your even being aware of it. Every time you sense anything at all, an electro-chemical connection is made in your brain. This connection leaves a trace or pathway between the neurons. Each one of these is, potentially, the beginnings of a memory. The more often that a particular pattern of connections is activated, the more likely it is that a memory will be created.

Memories can be of many different types. Most familiar are short-term memories, which get us through our everyday lives, and more deeply embedded long-term memories, but there are also categories such as implicit and explicit, procedural and declarative. These differentiate between, say, the memory of how to ride a bicycle and the memory involved in speaking a foreign language; memories that are facts, such as "Sinking of Titanic, 1912," and memories that allow us to find our way home every day. Much of the time these categories blur into each other and are interrelated.

There are three aspects to memory: creating it in the first place, storing it and recalling it. Each of these stages is affected by your emotional state, by your general health, by your degree of engagement and by a number of other factors that we do not yet fully understand.

Creating a memory

Our brains simply do not register, except in the most fleeting way, much of what we do or perceive. For if they stored trivia – what a passerby is wearing, the licence plate of the car in front of you – it is easy to imagine the whole memory system becoming clogged up.

Short-term memories describe those we aren't going to need to keep calling on in the future but which provide the very necessary prompts in our daily lives: what do you need to take to work with you this morning? Where are you going this evening? Information it is important to keep will be transferred into long-term memory.

Storing memories

You are able to cross a street safely by noticing and recalling the noise and sights that indicate the presence of cars. You recognize, from your memory of past experience, what a particular tone of voice conveys, such as happiness or anger. Many of your stored memories exist at an unconscious level, waiting to be summoned up in the future. As you get older your long-term memory tends to become clearer and your short-term memory may become less reliable.

Memories only have any validity if they can be retrieved, but your ability to do this is related to the effectiveness with which a memory is embedded in the first place. Learning how you can store memories is vital to the process of remembering.

Recalling memories

You meet a friend and remember their name, or a visit to an old haunt conjures up a host of memories. But recall can also be frustratingly elusive: the tune you can't remember the name of, that fourth thing you needed at the store. There are essentially three kinds of recall:

Straight recall	Information out of a memory store – for example, in a test or when you sing a song off by heart.
Recognition	Realizing you have encountered something before because you recognize it when you see, hear or read it again.
Reconstruction	Recreating a memory as you go along – the police use this type of recall in re-enacting a crime, hoping to jog the memories of witnesses.

Of course, the method you use to store and retrieve something will depend on what it is you are trying to recall – you would be unlikely to use the same technique for remembering where you left your spectacles as you would for remembering a historical fact. The exercises opposite show you how to create patterns and connections using mnemonic rhymes and devices. And the next few steps explore in more detail how you can imprint things more firmly in your memory and recall them when you need them.

EXERCISE 1: DIY Acrostics

Acrostics are those handy little phrases where the initial letters provide a memory jogger for something else: **R**ichard **O**f **Y**ork **G**ave **B**attle **I**n **V**ain for the first letters of the colours in the spectrum; **E**very **G**ood **B**oy **D**eserves **F**avour for the rising musical notes on a stave.

Make up your own acrostics to help fix facts or lists you wish you wouldn't keep forgetting. I remember the letters of my car's licence plate, S–FSG, as So Far So Good, increasingly appropriate as the car gets older!

EXERCISE 2: Memory Tags

The old trick of tying a knot in your handkerchief is a sort of tag, but a more memorable association is likely to work better. Try associating your friends' birthdays with their name: Jane Smith/April 5th - there are four letters in Jane and the fourth month is April; the letter S looks like the number 5.

Tags work particularly well for committing lists to memory. Practise memorizing your shopping list by making up a story to include all the items you need to buy, or phrase them so that they all begin with the same letter (fizzy water, fresh bread, food for cats...). Memory improves with practice, so do this regularly and you'll see how your success rate improves.

➤➤Step 4: Using Your Senses; Step 19: Big and Small Pictures

29 Making It Stick

It's so tempting to think of the brain as a kind of glorified filing cabinet, with drop folders just waiting to be filled with the events of your life. But the reality is much more complex. Even with today's brain imaging systems our knowledge of how the brain stores memories is relatively limited. All we really know is that many parts of the brain, including the hippocampus and the frontal lobes, have important roles to play in fixing a memory in our minds.

However, we do know that the brain does not just record events passively. As the four basic rules of memory opposite highlight, there are ways of influencing the likelihood of creating a memory that sticks. For example, a meaningless jumble of information is particularly difficult to remember. But if we can reorder a random series of events or facts into a pattern, then we add sense and make remembering easier.

We also retain information that we take in by more than one means. For example, it helps to write something down as well as say it out loud. And research has shown that we remember pictures better than words, so reinforcing a memory with a visual image helps to lodge it in our mind.

Emotions are important memory reinforcers, too (see page 106). Try the technique opposite that relates to the basic memory rules.

TECHNIQUE: Some Memory Rules

1 **We tend to remember the first and last items**

Break up study sessions so that you have lots of beginnings and endings.

Break up meetings into short items.

If you want someone to remember what you are saying, say it first or last!

Put your efforts into remembering middle sections of the data.

2 **Seeing patterns and connections helps**

Seek out connections in whatever you are learning. Create connections and patterns with mnemonics and rhymes (see pages 97 and 104).

Reorganize things so that you see the way they fit together. For example, you could summarize and group the key points of a lecture using your own headings or a Mind Map®.

3 **We remember odd things**

Create private (and odd!) links and/or unusual images to convert something ordinary or abstract into something striking and memorable (see pages 97 and 104).

4 **Regular practice or review helps**

Use regular repetition to embed something in your mind. So, if you want to memorize a list of key points, practise for 10 minutes every day for a week.

➤➤Step 19: Big and Small Pictures; Step 25: Mind Mapping®;
Step 37: Aging Well

30 Where, When, Why?

It's one thing to make a memory stick and another to recall it when you need it. Do you find yourself remembering friends' birthdays *after* the event? Or putting something in a secret place that becomes so secret that you cannot recall where it is?

Remembering is easier when you are not trying too hard. Feeling stressed has an adverse effect on memory, so take measures to relax. Try listening to a CD or tape that you know calms you down. Often sleeping on it really does work – go to bed telling yourself you want to recall something and see if it will come to you during the night or the next morning.

> *"Memory is the diary that we all carry around with us."*
> OSCAR WILDE (1854–1900)

One thing that helps a memory surface is a sensory trigger. Think of when a sudden smell or a particular noise has transported you back to a time in your past, or when memories have come flooding back on hearing a particular piece of music. You can use triggers like this to prompt recollection rather than just wait for the memory to pop into your mind unbidden.

Sight is one of our most powerful senses – as we have learned, we remember pictures more readily than what we read or hear. This next technique looks at ways in which you can reconstruct memories using vision as a trigger.

TECHNIQUE: Conjure Up Memories

To help you recall a memory, try to recreate the circumstances in which you originally stored it:

- Physically retrace your steps. This often works if you have walked into a room and forgotten what you came in for.
- Recreate the scene in your mind's eye, by "walking around" the situation as it originally was. This type of visualization takes concentration but you may be astonished at the small details you thought you had forgotten.

Using visual prompts when you consciously store a memory will help you when you want to retrieve it. For example:

- If you need to stop and ask a stranger for directions, try turning the instructions into a mental picture. For "Take the second turning off Kingly Street", you might picture a king wearing a crown embossed with the number 2. Later, conjuring up the visual image of the crown will be enough to trigger the direction.

➤➤ Step 4: Using Your Senses; Step 6: Relaxed Alertness; Step 22: Visualization

31 Who?

I remember one teacher at school who used to call everyone "Thingummy". Either he found it difficult to remember faces or, more probably, he chose not to as part of a certain affectation. But the result was the same. We all felt that he did not value us. Using people's names matters. That's why, for example, people are reduced to numbers in movies depicting hostile interrogation.

How easy do you find it to remember names and faces? Have you ever forgotten someone's name just moments after being introduced at a party? Or have you bumped into someone in the street and been unable to recall their name? Being able to put a name to a face is an important life skill. It can really help you to get on with people. It's the most effective way to show that someone has made an impact on you.

According to research carried out at the University of Sussex (UK), people are more likely to remember faces of their own race, age group or gender – remembering the familiar is easier. So, if we can identify a common characteristic or make a connection between someone else and ourselves, then that person becomes memorable.

Opposite are some tips for remembering people and their names in different circumstances. If you are really stuck, listen carefully for clues, such as other people using the name you have forgotten!

TECHNIQUE: Names and Faces

Try these approaches.

1 Notice odd details. Does the face have any unusual features? Is the nose long or bulbous? Are the eyes particularly feline or strikingly bright? Is the mouth rosebud-shaped or turned down? What about distinctive hair? But remember that hair colour and styles change! Now immediately associate these features with the person's name, saying to yourself "Sarah has a button-shaped nose" or "Ian has big ears."

2 Use words that start with the same letter to prompt your memory: Susan's scar, Harry's hairy head, Rachel's ringlets.

3 Use associations. Does the face remind you of anything? An animal? A movie star? A mood? Link the association to the name in your mind.

4 The moment you learn a name, use it and repeat it. Say "Good to meet you, Paul" not just "Good to meet you."

5 If you are in a meeting, make a seating plan with names. As the meeting goes on, see if you can learn everybody's name.

6 If you are going to be meeting a number of new people, perhaps at a business convention or a charity dinner, and you can get hold of a list of names beforehand, practise learning the names. Then when you meet someone, use the techniques above to link the name to the face. After the event, see how many faces and names you can recollect.

32 What?

Thirty days hath September,
April, June and November.
All the rest have thirty-one
Excepting February alone,
Which has twenty-eight days clear,
But twenty-nine in each Leap Year.

If only remembering all facts were as easy as remembering how many days there are in each month. This rhyme works because it combines lots of techniques for remembering facts: it uses repetition; the rhythm and rhyme act as clues; the first and the last facts stand out; the comparatively dull business of numbers of days in the months has been given added interest and meaning by being converted into a sing-song ditty.

In some ways remembering a fact all starts from the moment you first "meet" it. You need to engage with the fact, find a connection with it and invest it with some kind of meaning. Of course, not every fact that you need to learn can necessarily be put into a memorable rhyme. Sometimes you will need to force an association with something that you do find easy to recall. The techniques opposite call on the memory rules on page 99. Practise these, and remembering all sorts of facts can become second nature to you.

TECHNIQUE: Forget-it-not

1 **Repeat things you want to remember**

As soon as you hear a new word, fact or figure that you want to commit to memory, repeat it over and over in your head. When you learn about a new idea, go over it again later that day.

2 **Create clues or memory triggers**

Don't leave the data as a dry fact! Come up with an amusing or memorable association. Draw a picture. Make a rhyme or acronym or mnemonic – whatever helps trigger the original memory.

3 **Use the first and last to your advantage**

If you are trying to remember a number of things, identify the two most important elements and put one at the beginning and one at the end of any list you make. If you are trying to commit them to memory, make sure that they are the first and last thing you go over when you are looking at them.

4 **Find connections and patterns**

Find ways of making sense of whatever you are trying to memorize, whether it's a number, a date, or even just a word, by collecting together similar facts, creating a Mind Map®, making up a rhyme ("In 1492, Columbus sailed the ocean blue") – anything that will help you to make a connection with that particular item.

33 Feelings Matter

Feelings and memory are intimately connected. Think of where you were when you had your first kiss. Or what you were doing on 9/11 2001.

There are many myths about emotions, the most prevalent of which is the idea that there is one part of the brain alone which is responsible for them. But the more we understand the brain, the more we are realizing its complexity. Many components play a role in processing and responding to emotions – all helping to regulate our mood.

So how do feelings have an impact on your memory? Outrage, euphoria, desire, sorrow all give added meaning to what we are doing or what is happening around us at the time – which is why you probably remember that first kiss, where you were on 9/11, and so on.

Extreme negative emotions can have two opposite effects. They may sear an experience into your memory so that it seems to be ever there at a conscious level, or they may block it entirely as a protective measure. On a less extreme level, a negative emotion such as worry can make it more difficult to remember things, especially in the short term. If you can become more aware of your feelings, you can make them work for, not against, your ability to remember.

EXERCISE: Harnessing Your Emotions

Practise becoming more aware of your emotional responses to things.

In the past

Think back to your childhood. What are your happiest memories? What are your most painful ones? Is there any difference in the strength of these memories for you today? Ask yourself the same questions about memories over the past year.

Currently

What makes you happiest at home? And at work? How do your emotions tend to affect your recall of these situations? What causes you most distress at home and at work? Are there negative emotions you currently experience on a regular basis? How are they affecting your memory?

In the future

If you could learn to control one negative area of your emotional life, what would it be? How does it currently affect your performance? How would you like it to be different? Focus on that emotion. What words could you use to describe it? Can you visualize it? What sensations does it produce? Now distance yourself from the emotion. Feel the sensations gradually fading. Observe it as if it no longer belongs to you.

➤➤ Step 8: Overcoming Barriers; Step 22: Visualization

CHAPTER 6

Dealing with Change

Change is an inevitable part of the human condition. The seasons come and go. Unexpected things happen. New inventions are created. Yet many of us deal with change very badly.

In today's fast-moving world, this is partly because the rate of change is so rapid that we can hardly keep up with it. American social commentator Alvin Toffler describes this rate of change as "a totally new social force – a stream of change so accelerated that it influences our sense of time." Certainly there is something in this. Global trading, the Internet and digital technology mean that there is seemingly no time to stop and think.

Technological advances require us to keep developing our minds. What it takes to be smart depends on the kind of society you live in, but we need also to develop strategies for coping with the emotional effects of changes. In this chapter you will find out about some of the ways in which you need to deal with your feelings and change your behaviour and outlook if you want to be sufficiently adaptable to thrive in an uncertain world.

34 The Feelings of Change

You are all ready to go out and the phone rings: your friend has been taken ill and you are no longer able to go out for dinner together. Your company announces that it will be moving the office where you work to another city. Your partner who has been undertaking further study at a university starts to want to do different things and spend time with different people. Plans change. Things move on. People change. But how does it make you feel?

"It is not the strongest of the species that survive, nor the most intelligent, but the ones most responsive to change."
CHARLES DARWIN (1809-82)

Change brings emotions, often negative ones to begin with. When things are certain and predictable, we have an easy life. We follow safe routines and stick to well-trodden pathways. But the world we live in is not static, fixed or definite. We are constantly challenged by the uncertain or the new, and whenever this happens we have, in a sense, to start again. We discover something and find that it leads us to ask more questions. And the more we know about something, the more likely we are to see its complexities.

As humans evolved, there were good reasons why change should invoke strong feelings: the sudden disappearance of a source of food or a dramatic change in the weather were life-threatening situations that our ancestors needed to react to. Strong feelings stimulated their necessary reactions and ensured survival. Today, we may face different changes, but we still need to be just as responsive, using all our senses and our problem-solving abilities to deal with change.

The strength of our feelings about change tends to depend on two things: the seriousness of the change and the degree to which it has been forced upon us rather than chosen. In most cases of involuntary change, the feelings we have follow a pattern:

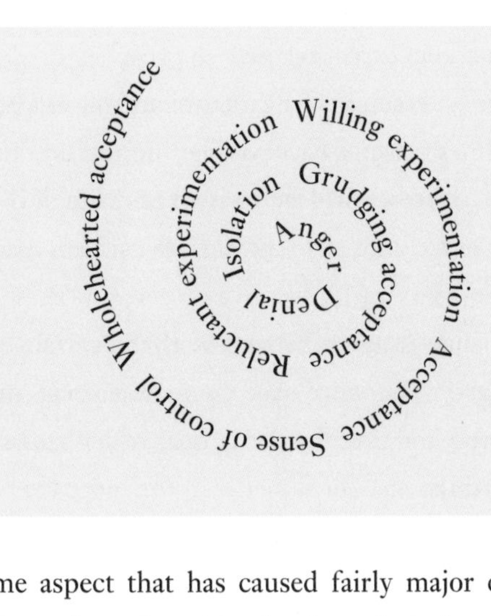

Take some aspect that has caused fairly major change in your life recently and see how closely the spiral above describes the feelings you experienced. How did you feel when you first found out that something was changing? Most people feel a degree of anger. There is often a strong sense of injustice and the most obvious reaction is to rail against this. The next common reaction is to choose, consciously or unconsciously, not to deal with the situation, preferring to hope it will go away. This can leave you feeling very isolated, especially if others around you appear to be coping well.

As you became more fully aware of the situation and began to accept the reality of what was happening, you probably – albeit reluctantly – started to test the waters. Did you try responding to the new situation, exploring new approaches or doing things differently? In most cases, as you experiment, you will begin to find new and sometimes better ways of doing things. Did this make you feel much better, happy even? Having worked through your negative emotions, did you feel more in control of the situation and ready to embrace the change?

Of course, change is not as formulaic as the spiral suggests. It's much more messy. But once you come to expect this kind of emotional journey, it is much easier to deal with change that seems difficult and threatening.

➤➤Step 13: Keeping Going; Step 21: Finding the Problem; Step 26: Clarifying; Step 33: Feelings Matter; Step 51: Setting Goals

TECHNIQUE: Facing the Challenge of Change

Try these suggestions to help you deal with some of the feelings of change.

- Name your feelings. There's a temptation to keep your feelings to yourself. But it is much more helpful to recognize and name your feelings. Ask yourself what has made you feel this way and start to talk to friends and family about the issues that emerge.
- Be specific. Pinpoint the aspect of change that is causing negative feelings. Allowing fear or anger or sadness to affect all areas of your life can render you incapable of action. Don't lose a sense of perspective.
- Connect to the past. There's very little that is completely new in life. Think of similar situations and how you successfully coped with them in the past.
- Be true to yourself. Change is unsettling and can lead you to question yourself, but remember, although external events may have changed, you are still the same person, with your own identity and past.
- Develop a plan of action. The sooner you do this, the sooner you will engage your mind in coming up with creative ways ahead, and this will help you to regain a sense of control. Try to give yourself lots of choices. Remember, just two options present you with a dilemma; more than two and you have a choice.

35 Changing Behaviour

Why might you want to change the way you behave? There are lots of reasons. If you smoke, over-eat or have an obviously static lifestyle, then you might want to change in order to become healthier and improve your quality of life. Or if you tend to stick to the same routines, then you might want to inject variety and freshness into your life – for example, changing your route to work, your usual vacation destination or your relaxation activities.

You might also wish to change ingrained habits. We all get used to saying and doing things in certain ways. And it's so easy to slip into patterns of behaviour: your partner asks you something and you snap back at them; something breaks down or will not work properly and you become enraged, and so on. Or you might want to change a belief you have held for a long time because you recognize that it is leading you to behave in ways which you (or other people) do not like.

If you are in an unchallenging job or an unsatisfactory relationship or if you are harbouring a vague sense of unfulfilment, then your motivation for change may be more subtle, arising from a desire to make yourself happier.

Sometimes change is imposed on you and you have no choice but to react to external events. For example, the arrival of a child brings new priorities and means that you can't stick with many of your previous routines. Changing your behaviour in the light of the circumstances is essential if you are to use your mind effectively.

Take heart! All these changes are possible to achieve. From the earliest age when you do something which leads to negative consequences, you learn to modify your behaviour – you accidentally touch a hot radiator and hastily withdraw your hand. This does not just apply to physical actions. Learned behaviour equally influences what we say, what we do and how we react in almost every conceivable situation.

"Everyone thinks of changing the world, but no one thinks of changing himself."
LEO TOLSTOY (1828–1910)

Until comparatively recently, little was known about the significant degree to which it was possible to change behaviour. Indeed, there was a school of thought, sometimes referred to as behaviourism, which argued that certain kinds of behaviour are almost impossible to change. However, many of our most important institutions – for example, schools and prisons – are founded on the assumption that it is possible to change behaviour. Advertisers, counsellors, parents and politicians all engage a lot of effort in changing people's behaviour. And you, too, need to believe that change is possible if you want to carry on boosting your mind so that it will adapt when it needs to.

To help you do this, it is useful to look at changing an aspect of how you behave as a four-step process.

First, you need to recognize the issue. Noticing that something needs changing might involve a sudden realization or it might dawn on you as the result of feedback from others. You may want to analyze your behaviour further to help you learn when you behave a certain way and what tends to trigger this.

Second, you have to *want* to change and take an active decision to do so. At the heart of all this are your values and beliefs: if you believe that it does not matter how much you smoke or eat, then you are unlikely to change your habits. The same is true of behaviour that affects other people: if you really want to avoid losing your temper, then you need to believe that self-control matters and that the feelings of those around you are important, too.

Third, to turn words into actions you need a concrete plan, ideally with milestones built into it so that you can keep yourself motivated. Ensure your timescale is realistic – entrenched behaviour cannot normally be changed overnight, so expect and plan for setbacks along the way!

Fourth, you need to commit to the plan: you are much more likely to stick to your plan if you write it down and confide in a few close friends or family members, who can prompt and encourage you if you slip up.

TECHNIQUE: **Behaving Better**

Use the four-step process to try and change an aspect of your behaviour that you are unhappy with. As an example, let's suppose that your anger is negatively affecting your relationships at home and at work.

1 Recognize the issue. Perhaps your partner has remarked on your temper or someone you work with has suggested that your anger is unhelpful. Try to be clear about *what* makes you angry. Something breaking down? Someone missing a deadline? Then, explore *why* you are angry. Are you stressed? Has anger become a habitual response?
2 Decide to change. Make a list of your reasons, such as "because it's ruining my relationships"; "because it makes me look ridiculous"; "because I do not like myself for it." This will help you to clarify why you need to take action.
3 Make a plan. Your plan could be as simple as slowly counting to 10 or deliberately thinking of something funny every time you feel your anger rising. You could also ask those close to you to give you an early warning signal if you are showing signs of your old behaviour.
4 Commit to the plan. Remember to write down your plan and tell people close to you what you are trying to do so that they can support you.

➤➤Step 9: Adjusting Attitudes; Step 13: Keeping Going; Step 41: Giving and Receiving Feedback; Step 51: Setting Goals

36 Moving On

It was the Irish playwright George Bernard Shaw who remarked that "Reasonable people adapt themselves to the world. Unreasonable people attempt to adapt the world to themselves. All progress, therefore, depends on unreasonable people." And there is a grain of truth in this. Often, for progress to be achieved, the world needs people who see beyond conventional wisdom and think difficult and challenging thoughts.

Swiss psychologist Jean Piaget first suggested that we learn through a process of adaptation. You notice something, adjust your thinking and, as a consequence, adapt the way you act, and move on. Piaget used two contrasting words for this, "accommodation" and "assimilation". In practice, you either adapt your theory to your experience – accommodation – or you fit your experience to any theory you have already formed in your head – assimilation.

So, let's say your theory of management is that all managers are incompetent and you meet one who is highly skilled and effective. You can either accommodate your views by adjusting your theory: managers now become capable of competent or incompetent behaviour. Or you can chose to assimilate this data: your view of managers remains the same and your mind explains your experience by thinking of the good manager as an exception to the rule.

Of the two kinds of adaptation described by Piaget, accommodation is the more challenging, because it requires you to rethink the way you view the world. Effective thinkers recognize that accommodation is a way in which they can change and adapt their world-view in the light of new evidence.

When change is particularly challenging, you may need to work a bit harder to be able to move on from it. Two common examples of this are the break-up of a marriage or long-term relationship and the experience of being made redundant from your job. The notion of assimilation does not go far enough in explaining what is going on in these situations. This is because the experience has gone against our most basic beliefs. We thought we would be with that one person forever, but now we know we won't. We thought we were secure in our job, but now we've unexpectedly lost it. We cannot make our experience fit our theory because the difference is too great to reconcile in our minds.

Accommodation can help in such a situation, but it means going beyond the bounds of the kinds of accommodation that you may be used to. If you can draw on your ability to recast your ways of looking at things, you are much more likely to find a way of dealing with a drastic change in your life. A situation involving such a full-frontal challenge to your self-esteem requires you to use your mind in a really powerful way to be able to move on.

One good way of doing this is to use the idea of a story. When you stop and think about it, your mind uses stories every day. Even the "How was your day?" question over supper is likely to lead to one. Whenever you try to remember how you did something in the past, you will probably produce some kind of narrative. And when someone asks you what you do for a living, it is not difficult to start to tell a story about yourself. For example, I might say, "I'm a writer and motivational speaker," before going on to elaborate on this bald description by telling mini-stories to illustrate what I mean.

When you tell a story about yourself, you are in control. You are shaping things, putting your spin on events. If something challenging has happened to you, one of the most effective things you can do is to establish a clear and helpful story in your own mind. So, "We've decided to go our separate ways as we had just stopped making each other happy," can be a helpful account of a broken relationship, even if one of you is more responsible than the other. Or, "I used to work for widget.com, but we were taken over by globalgreed.com and I lost my job," saves you having to explain your part in any incompetent management which may have been a contributory factor in your redundancy. The following exercise will give you practice at putting a positive spin on a tricky situation.

➤➤Step 7: Being Half Full; Step 13: Keeping Going; Step 26: Clarifying

EXERCISE: Get Your Story Straight

Unless you find yourself currently dealing with something that is really challenging you, you may need to think of an imaginary situation. Or practise by thinking of something that has happened to you in the past and use it as the stimulus.

1 Find yourself somewhere quiet and comfortable to sit that is free from distractions. Take a few deep breaths.
2 Think about the situation confronting you. How is it currently making you feel? If someone asked you to describe it, what would you say? Are you comfortable with your description? Or does it somehow put you in a bad light or make you feel victimized?
3 Now try framing what has happened in a way that makes you feel more in control of the situation, and is less damaging to your self-esteem. It may help you to think of two different kinds of listener, one formal (an interviewer, perhaps) and one casual (someone you meet at a party). Try:
   - to be true to yourself
   - not to take the blame for things beyond your control
   - to express at least one positive angle or outcome
   - to come up with various explanations for what has happened.

Now practise your story so that you are ready to tell it to yourself and others – so that you are ready to move on.

37 Aging Well

Have you ever experienced one of those "senior moments" – for example, when you've lost the thread of what you were saying, mid-sentence? Or are you worried about whether your parents, or yourself, will cope in old age?

Perhaps you have heard the saying, "Use it or lose it". While meant as a well-intentioned reminder of the need to stay mentally active, for some people this saying has become a gentle threat of mental deterioration. However, the idea that unless you use your brain it will wither away is only partially true. While it is certainly the case that from an early age we all experience "neural pruning" (the elimination of excess capacity in the brain), there is still plenty left for you to work with, so you don't need to panic!

Latest thinking suggests two key stages in the aging process. The first, at around 50, is when your brain begins to lose some of its power to make new connections. And the second occurs about 20 years later when you may find it harder to retrieve memories. But this doesn't mean that the aging process *begins* at 50, so the sooner you start looking after your brain, the better. The best way to do this is to stay active – this involves exercising both your body and your brain.

➤➤Step 5: Staying Healthy in Mind and Body

TECHNIQUE: Active Habits

Try some of these suggestions to help you develop active habits to boost your mind power.

- Read widely. Experiment with different genres – for example, mix fiction and non-fiction, and ensure that you have always got a book on the go. Join your local library. You might also like to join a book group to encourage you to actively discuss your reading matter on a regular basis.
- Keep physically active. If going to the gym or playing tennis or golf isn't for you, join a walking group, or learn tai chi or yoga or even belly-dancing.
- Be socially active. Try new activities where you will be learning new skills as well as meeting new people, and pass on skills you have learned to others.
- Keep travelling. New places act as a powerful stimulus to the brain.
- Tease your brain. Do puzzles, crosswords and quizzes. Try this famous puzzle to get your juices flowing: see if you can join up all of the dots with four straight lines and without lifting your pen from the paper. (Answer on page 176.)

● ● ●

● ● ●

● ● ●

CHAPTER 7

Effective Communication

You may have the best ideas and the most analytical mind in the world. But unless you can communicate what you are thinking, you will find it very difficult to fulfill your potential and almost impossible to persuade other people to your point of view.

Often we think we have communicated when all we have actually done is told someone something. This is particularly the case since the invention of email, whereby pressing the "send" button it is possible to delude oneself that communication has taken place! But the process of communication is two-way. How can you be sure that your message has even been read by the recipient?

In this chapter you will learn how to keep things simple and clear and you will learn about the power of listening. We will also explore what happens when you need to disagree with those around you, and discover the value of feedback.

38 Explaining Clearly

Think about the number of times you have been frustrated by poor explanations. A set of instructions is imprecise and you waste hours figuring out how to get something to work. The purpose of a meeting is not clearly explained and those attending grow irritated.

In a famous experiment, Ellen Langer, an American psychology professor, showed something very surprising about the power of one word, "because". She asked researchers to see if they could jump a Xerox machine queue at work. The question: "Excuse me, I have five pages, may I use the Xerox machine?" proved 60 percent successful. Whereas: "Excuse me, I have five pages, may I use the Xerox machine because I am in a rush?" was 94 percent successful.

Langer also tried a third question: "Excuse me, I have five pages, may I use the Xerox machine because I have to make some copies?" Although no real reason is given here, this approach was 93 percent successful. Langer showed that offering some kind of explanation, especially using the word "because", is a smart move: it persuades people to respond graciously and helps you get things done.

Imagine you are explaining a business proposal to a client or some homework to a child. Your explanation is likely to involve more than a single sentence, yet you still want it to be clear. Investing time in learning how to explain issues will be well worth it.

TECHNIQUE: How to Explain Yourself

Try these six prompt questions when you are preparing an explanation.

1. What do you want the other person to know, or what do they want to know? Consider the other person's point of view and don't overload them.
2. How much do they already know? Don't patronize. Try to gauge the level of understanding – if appropriate, do some research.
3. What's the main point you are trying to make? Cut to the chase. Differentiate between what is essential and what is optional.
4. What else is important? Would additional information make your explanation clearer – perhaps a similar example, an analogy or a common saying?
5. How will you deal with the feelings involved? Be aware of how what you are saying may affect people. Don't expect a surprised or shaken recipient to take in every detail. If it directly affects them (but not you), allow them time to process what you are saying.
6. What kind of language should you use? If you need to use technical vocabulary because of your subject matter or audience, do so. But assume that a shorter word is usually better than a longer one! Also think about the tone of what you are saying.

➤➤ Step 26: Clarifying; Step 41: Giving and Receiving Feedback; Step 43: Walking in Other People's Shoes

39 Listening Carefully

The American poet Robert Frost once wrote: "Education is the ability to listen to almost anything without losing your temper or your self-confidence." Listening is a smart strategy and one that too few people adopt. How many times in a typical day do you find yourself unable to finish your sentence because someone interrupts you? Are you guilty of interrupting others, too?

"When you talk, you repeat what you already know; when you listen, you often learn something."

JARED SPARKS (1789–1866)

When it comes to getting the best out of your mind, there are a number of compelling reasons why you might want to listen more and talk less. By the simple act of listening, you pick up other people's good ideas. And you can make a mental note not to use their sillier ones! You'll also be able to see things from other people's points of view. Too many people go through life never really knowing what people around them think because they have simply never made the time to stop and ask.

People will warm to you if you make an effort to listen, because listening is seen as a mark of respect, and those who listen tend to be trusted more. By listening, rather than immediately answering back, you are more likely to keep your cool, for you have built in "waiting time". And remember, listening is much faster than talking!

TECHNIQUE: How to Become a Better Listener

Try the following suggestions to help you improve your listening skills.

- Maintain eye contact with the speaker whenever possible.
- Focus on what someone is saying, not how they are saying it. It's easy to get distracted by a distinctive accent, tone of voice or vocal quirks.
- Make sure you show that you're interested and that you are following what is being said by making quiet acknowledging sounds.
- Be patient and avoid jumping in with too many questions.
- Check your understanding of what is being said from time to time by repeating things back and encouraging the speaker to add more details.
- Pick up on non-verbal cues. Open hand gestures may suggest that a response from you would be helpful. Not meeting your gaze may indicate that the person is not ready for you to interject.
- Try to empathize. Draw the speaker out. Encourage them to tell you more by saying things such as "I guess this may have made you feel..."
- Try not to let your mind wander. Stay active by asking yourself questions about what you are listening to.
- Treat listening as a challenging mental task and feel good because you are managing to achieve it.

➤➤Step 18: Deferring Judgment; Step 41: Giving and Receiving Feedback; Step 43: Walking in Other People's Shoes

40 How to Disagree

It is easy to see why many people find disagreeing so disagreeable. We all want to be liked, and for some people this desire is so strong that they will avoid disagreements at all costs.

Perhaps we should not be surprised that conflict is difficult to manage. At a deeply instinctive level human beings have survived by reacting in starkly simplistic ways. When faced with conflict, we are programmed either to flee or to fight. And, to take one example, many prime-time radio or television political interviews today exemplify how raw aggression and plain rudeness can provide such unattractive examples of how not to disagree. But while avoiding disagreements may, at first, seem like a desirable character trait, it can actually limit our ability to discover new things. Without a clash in the arena of science and politics we might not know that the Earth is round or that AIDS is a largely manageable condition.

There are lots of reasons why we disagree with people. We may think that someone is mistaken. We may consider that something which is presented as the only way ahead is actually one of many options. We may find arguments too emotional or too partial. Or, while we may accept the premise of a position, we may not go along with the conclusions that are drawn from it. So, we cannot always avoid disagreements, but we *can* learn how to handle them smartly.

EXERCISE: Disagree with Style

If you want to get good at disagreeing, you will need to practise. Ask a friend or family member to help you. Choose a topic that is contentious – for example, a current political, environmental or social issue. Take opposing views of it and try using the following techniques to argue your case.

- Show that you respect the other person's opinion.
- Be polite and point out errors of fact without being rude.
- Use statistics and examples to back up your argument.
- Offer alternative explanations.
- Use humour when you need to lighten things up. Poking fun at yourself can help to ease the tension and is unlikely to offend anyone!
- Remember to maintain your cool. The more emotional you feel yourself becoming, the more you may want to pause and wait before you speak.

Try some of these phrases in your disagreement exercise:

"I take a slightly different view..."

"You're right but..."

"That's one way of looking at it..."

"I see what you mean but..."

"I am not sure that the issue is quite that simple..."

➤➤ Step 15: Pause for Thought; Step 21: Finding the Problem; Step 38: Explaining Clearly; Step 47: Dealing with Conflict

41 Giving and Receiving Feedback

"Make sure you have someone in your life from whom you can get reflective feedback," says the American management guru Warren Bennis. Without feedback you remain doomed to make the same mistakes on a daily basis. Feedback arms you with useful information and, if you can accept and act on that information, then you will learn from your mistakes and develop your ability to learn.

Let's imagine you are living life to the full, but as a consequence you rarely seem to have time to see your partner or your family, and when you do, you are so tired that you are endlessly grumpy. A close friend, seeing what is going on, picks a good moment to offer you some feedback.

She gently mentions that she has seen your partner looking distressed and is worried about your relationship. She wonders whether it is really necessary to work quite such long hours. Nothing in what your friend is saying is at all critical or malicious, she is simply holding up a mirror to you. And you do not like what you see. Although it causes you uncomfortable reflection, some of which makes you angry and defensive, you resolve to make a few significant changes in your life.

Receiving feedback can work like this in all aspects of your life. Sometimes it is effective because it brings something to your attention which you have stopped noticing, as in the example you have just read. It acts as a jolt to your system and helps to prevent things going so badly wrong that they are irreparable.

At other times feedback is helpful after the event, especially when something has not gone as well as you expected. Unfortunately, in this type of situation, receiving feedback can also be difficult as no one likes to feel that they have failed, and feedback after failure can feel like an extra blow. But you need to remind yourself that mistakes are an important part of the learning process.

There are all sorts of reasons why giving feedback can be difficult. You may be very close to someone and fear that what you say may threaten your friendship, the person to whom you need to give feedback may be your boss, or you may suspect that you are likely to get an emotional response and be in for a stormy ride.

360° feedback

Some organizations have realized the huge value of feedback and have introduced something called 360° feedback. As its name suggests, this means feedback from all quarters: from the person you work for, from your colleagues, from those who work for you, and from clients or customers. Feedback like this has several benefits. First, it helps you to see yourself as others see you. Second, it provides you with specific ideas on how you can improve.

And third, it enables you to give out powerful positive messages about yourself. Asking other people to tell you what they think about you suggests that you are the kind of person who wants to learn from your mistakes, that you are open to criticism and that you value the opinions of those around you. And there's nothing to stop you asking for feedback from all members of your own family, too!

TECHNIQUE 1: **How to Receive Feedback**

Before you receive feedback from someone, run through the following prompts.

- Check that you are ready to receive it. If you just need a few moments to get into the right frame of mind, buy some time by taking a bathroom break or fetching a glass of water. But if you are feeling vulnerable or irritable, explain that now is not a good time and set another definite time instead.
- Try to listen rather than jump in with an immediate justification.
- Try to stay calm!
- Thank the person for giving you the feedback – it may have been hard for them, too.

➤➤ Step 16: Taking Stock; Step 17: Mistakes Are Good; Step 38: Explaining Clearly; Step 39: Listening Carefully; Step 43: Walking in Other People's Shoes

TECHNIQUE 2: How to Give Feedback

When you need to offer feedback, try my **SAQ** approach.

S Be **S**pecific. Concentrate on a particular moment or incident. Focus on what it was that you observed. Describe what you saw or thought or felt. Be constructive. Suggest some ways in which the person might like to think about the incident, and how they might deal with the situation from this point onward.

A Make sure what you say is **A**ctionable. For example, it's not very helpful to tell someone to get better at dealing with email if they do not have access to a networked computer.

Q Be **Q**uick. Try to give feedback as close to the event as possible. If too much time goes by, your comments can seem irrelevant, irritating or petty. And if you don't give early feedback, it's easy for both of you to move on and forget the things that have gone wrong.

It's also helpful to consider the following pointers.

- Make sure you focus on behaviour and not on personality.
- Check that the recipient is ready and able to receive feedback. (It may not be a good moment if they are under pressure or about to dash off to an appointment.)
- Prepare at least two specific and genuine compliments, which you can give before you say things that may be seen as critical.

42 Public Speaking

Have you ever suffered a sleepless night because you have to give a speech at work the next day? Or fretted about a family occasion that's coming up when you will have to say a few words? Most of us have done this. It's natural to be nervous about standing up in public.

What's going on in your mind when you speak in public? The simple answer is that there are two conflicting forces at work: you are using your *rational* mind to string your words together coherently, but at the same time your *emotional* mind is engaged. All attention is focused on you and you feel exposed and stressed. Consequently, many people freeze up and find the experience of public speaking distressing and difficult. Preparation is the key to conquering stage fright, and the techniques opposite will help you with the different elements of preparation. When it comes to delivering your speech, take deep breaths and have some water to hand. And if you can, make eye contact with your audience. After the event, ask for feedback and make a note of anything you would like to do differently next time while it is fresh in your mind.

➤➤ Step 25: Mind Mapping®; Step 28: The Making of Memories; Step 29: Making It Stick; Step 31: Who?; Step 32: What?; Step 41: Giving and Receiving Feedback

CHECKLIST: How to Prepare a Speech

Use the following hints to help you prepare a successful speech.

- Find out who your audience will be and for how long you are due to speak.
- Decide your content and order. Keep it simple and focus on a few key messages. You could use a Mind Map® to help you brainstorm your main points. Memorize key words or make yourself some prompt cards with headings on them.
- Concentrate on the beginning and end of your speech. Good ways of starting include introducing yourself and giving a brief overview of what you are going to say, telling a short, funny and relevant story to grab your audience's attention or making a specific connection with the place you are in or the people you are talking to. Write out your first two sentences so that you are confident about the start. A one-sentence summary is a pretty good way to end your speech, making sure you finish on a positive note.
- Use the four rules of memory in Step 29 to fix key points in your mind.
- If you need to remember names, facts or statistics, use Steps 31 and 32 to help you.
- Decide whether you are going to use any visual aids, such as flip charts or video clips. These will build in variety and act as memory prompts, too.
- Practise delivering your speech in front of a mirror or to a friend, and time yourself as you do so.

CHAPTER 8

Effective Negotiating

To be a success in life it is not enough to be individually smart. You also need to be able to persuade other people of your abilities. And this means developing first-rate negotiating skills.

Perhaps you believe that you have the most brilliant mind in the world and can see what the smartest course of action is in any circumstance. Unfortunately, not everyone agrees with you. In fact, others seem either to disagree with you frequently or dismiss your opinion altogether. Might there be a grain of truth in this for you? If so, you will find this chapter especially helpful.

In the next few steps you will learn about the power of empathy and how to anticipate what other people may be thinking and feeling. This chapter will also help you understand more about the two-way nature of relationships and how to influence people to get your way so that everyone feels that they have won. It won't always be easy. But even where there is conflict, you can get better at dealing with it.

43 Walking in Other People's Shoes

There is a Native American proverb that you should not judge another person until you have walked "two moons in their moccasins." In other words, before you can have an opinion about someone else you need to have seen things from their perspective. The simple word for this is empathy, the capacity for seeing another person's point of view and imagining what they might be feeling.

In today's egocentric society it is all too easy to see things from only one perspective – your own. But this is not an endearing characteristic! Being able to empathize helps you to make and keep friends, see solutions that others cannot see, win arguments and come up with creative ideas.

If you wish to make friends, listening and questioning may be more helpful than talking about yourself. If you are trying to understand why your son is crying, then you may need to come down to his level (literally) and see what it is he has bumped his head on. If you are attempting to win someone over, then you may need to show that you have their interests at heart, too. And if you are trying to come up with great ideas, you may need to see if you can let go of your own selfish needs.

➤➤Step 39: Listening Carefully; Step 41: Giving and Receiving Feedback

EXERCISE: How Do They See It?

Try the following three approaches. In each case, practise saying "I bet (s)he is thinking/feeling..." and see how often you can complete the sentence.

Role-play

Spend 10 minutes swapping roles with a good friend as you do something typical together – for example, going for a walk, shopping, visiting a café or gallery. See if you can adopt each other's gestures, tone and movements. How did it go? Ask each other for feedback.

Close observation

Choose a time where you can observe someone in a tricky situation. A good example is a meeting where you can watch someone under pressure but do not have to participate much yourself, or a dinner party where someone is engaged in a heated conversation. Watch the person closely. How do they convey their point and respond to questions? Imagine how a friend might act in this person's position. Recount the scenario to your friend and see how close you came.

Reading the newspaper

Choose a news report and, as you read it, try to imagine what different people mentioned in it might be thinking. For example, if your report covers a severe storm, how might a local business person, a parent, and a tourist be feeling? Do their viewpoints vary? What are the differing concerns and implications?

44 Two-way Relationships

The more you give, the more you receive. Whether you are thinking about your partner, your friends or those you work with, this principle holds well. And when it comes to improving your mind, there is a very real sense in which two or more minds are better than one. The more you can make every relationship an active two-way one, the more you will have access to other people's ideas.

If you want a relationship to be successful, then you need to invest in it. Above all, this means understanding the needs of the other person. Giving someone a bunch of flowers can be pretty futile if what they really want is to spend time with you to talk things through.

"Give and it will be given to you."

ST LUKE 6:38

Take a moment to think about an important relationship in your life. If you have to think hard to recall the last time you showed that person that you really value them, then your relationship may not be as two-way as it should be!

So, what steps can you take to show someone that you value them and that you are making an effort to understand their needs?

Well, first, you need to make them feel noticed. Feeling invisible is not much fun. Try observing and then commenting on gestures, actions, clothes, new habits – anything that tells you more about the person. Second, share your time. Some people have the knack of doing this even when they are busy. It's something to to do with the quality of attention you give someone even if you have lots of other things to do. Giving just 10 minutes of your full, undivided attention is often better than several hours of half-hearted company.

Third, offer your help before you are asked. If you can anticipate someone's needs, your actions will be even more appreciated. This can be something as simple as offering to go to the supermarket if your partner is running late after a hectic day, or preparing notes for a meeting before your time-pressured colleague or boss requests them. But be realistic in taking on obligations to others. You can make things worse if you make a promise which you cannot deliver.

It is not only giving that is important: the way you respond to someone else's efforts affects your relationship, too. Be gracious when you accept gifts or help of any kind. Many people feel awkward receiving compliments, and can end up making the giver feel awkward, too or, worse, making them wish they hadn't bothered. If you can practise some suitable replies, such as saying, "It's kind of you to say so" or "I'm glad you think so", then you can prevent yourself from rejecting the compliment. This will ensure you give the donor the pleasure that can go with giving.

➤➤Step 18: Deferring Judgment; Step 39: Listening Carefully; Step 43: Walking in Other People's Shoes

45 Influencing Others

Have you ever wished you could get your boss to agree to your suggestions more readily? Or wondered how to persuade your partner to come around to your way of thinking? Or perhaps you feel that you have lost authority with your children, who always seem to be able to twist you around their little finger when they want something? Most people would like to be better at influencing others, and if this is true of you, you may want to read the next few pages very carefully.

Give and take

Why do people give you free samples in supermarkets? Why do magazines frequently have free gifts attached to them? Why do free mints often appear at the end of dinner in a restaurant? Because in all these situations, by appearing to give something for nothing, the giver confers a sense of responsibility. It's called the reciprocity principle: you scratch my back and I'll scratch yours!

Most of us have engaged in some deliberate horse-trading at some stage: for example, "If you help me with the washing up, I'll drive you into town." But the reciprocity principle can be used in more subtle ways, too. For example, what happens when your son or daughter makes you a cup of tea without your asking? You feel good and you're more likely to grant them a favour the next time they ask. Think about how this might work in reverse – how doing someone a favour without an obvious comeback can reap benefits.

Try asking

Often all you need to do is ask. By the simple act of asking a question you tend to engage the listener in seeking to solve your problem with you and inevitably they tend to come around to your view of the world. Telephone sales staff use this tactic all the time. Have you ever felt you would like to help homeless children? Do you fancy taking a short break and finishing what you are doing later? Just by asking you can start a dialogue with someone and subtly suggest your agenda.

The next time you want to persuade someone to do something, jot down some carefully prepared questions that will encourage them to see things from your perspective.

The contrast factor

When you emerge from a theatre matinée, the early evening seems bright. If you put your hand in icy water, then even luke-warm water feels hot afterwards. Using contrast can help you win an argument or get your way. Shop assistants understand the value of contrast. This is why they ask if you want to buy a tin of polish when you have just purchased a pair of expensive new shoes. After spending a lot of money, the polish seems like a bargain! And why do real-estate agents bother to take you to a house that doesn't meet any of your criteria? It's because you'll be so relieved when you see something halfway decent that you'll want to snap it up!

Try this tactic when you want to ask for a favour from someone. First, ask them for something really big that you do not need and know they cannot grant you. Then go for what you really want. They are much more likely to grant you your wish.

Feeling good

Think about the people you know who always seem to get their own way. The chances are that they have one thing in common: they all know the value of making you feel good about yourself, especially if they are about to ask you a favour. Most of us respond well to flattery. If you are told that you look good or are congratulated on your work or are paid almost any compliment that is realistic and believable, your self-esteem rises. You feel better about yourself. And good feelings somehow seem to rub off. If someone makes you feel good, you are more likely to do their bidding.

➤➤ Step 38: Explaining Clearly; Step 44: Two-way Relationships; Step 46: Win-win Solutions

TECHNIQUE: How to Get Your Own Way

When it comes to getting your own way, first, it is important to be clear about what you want. Then there are a number of possible approaches which you might take. Here are some for you to try.

- Offer a bargain. Work out what is in it for the other person. If possible, make a small concession, so they will feel more compelled to give you what you want.
- Make an appeal to the emotions. Use phrases such as "If you were able to help me just this once I'd be so grateful to you."
- Flatter the person you are trying to persuade, but remember to be realistic and genuine.
- Give a clear explanation. Saying "because" rather than just making a demand improves your power of persuasion.
- Ask for a difficult or big favour first, possibly something that you do not actually expect to get. Then introduce the request for what you really want.
- Get their commitment to helping you to get a good result before you seek to persuade them.
- Have some evidence ready to add authenticity to your case.
- Use language that you know will be understood.
- Be polite, listen and empathize. This will help you establish a good relationship with the other person, making them less likely to refuse your request.

46 Win-win Solutions

While the phrase "win-win" is a recent arrival in the management lexicon, the thinking behind it is a lot older and more substantial. Whether you are buying or selling or trying to persuade someone to do something, it is often smarter for both parties to feel that they have won. When you are thinking creatively or trying to solve a problem, you are often better off collaborating than competing.

Imagine this scenario. A group of about 30 people are told to get into pairs facing each other. Each person grasps their partner's right hand at shoulder height. The aim of the game is to see how many times you can force your opponent's hand on to their shoulder in a form of arm-wrestling in just 30 seconds.

Most pairs wrestle away, recording a few hits and emitting lots of grunts! But one pair work together. They move their hands between each other's shoulders like a clock pendulum, recording the same high number of hits on each other! They have spotted the challenge for what it really is – a veiled invitation to be smart and collaborate.

It is amazing how often we find that our minds are set on a competitive approach. Perhaps, at a deep level, we fear that there is only a minority of winners. But whatever your goal, it is almost always possible to find a solution which suits you and the person or people with whom you are dealing.

TECHNIQUE: Everyone's a Winner

Use these prompts to practise how you might go about achieving a win-win solution next time you need it.

Ask yourself:

- What do I want? What will make me feel good?
- If I get what I want, how will the other person feel?
- If what I am planning to do will make the other person feel bad (and less likely to agree to it), what might make the other person feel good (and more likely to agree to it)?

Try to:

- Clarify the other person's needs and goals and convey that you will make an effort to achieve them.
- Be seen to seek a compromise. This will create a climate of cooperation and encourage the other person to listen to your wishes and give in to your demands.
- Whenever you think you only have two choices, one that is good for you and one that is bad, try to think of a third (and fourth) option which might suit both parties.

➤➤Step 21: Finding the Problem; Step 24: What If?; Step 26: Clarifying; Step 45: Influencing Others

47 Dealing with Conflict

Some people seem to court conflict: there's something about almost everything that they say which seems to raise the blood pressure of those around them. You do not want to be like this! Some people seem to have a very short fuse: the tiniest thing seems to upset them, rendering their minds ineffective until they have calmed down. Neither do you want to be like this!

If you can deal with conflict effectively, you will stop wasting your efforts in unnecessary arguments. You will be able to deal with complex situations better because you will have more energy to invest in them and both your emotional and your rational minds will be more likely to be working in harmony. And, if you stop reacting negatively to criticism, and see it as a helpful source of feedback instead, then you'll learn more about yourself.

Of course, there will be moments in everyone's life when the conflict is so serious that it is not easy to see how it can ever be resolved. But if you are prepared to try to understand each other's point of view, then progress can be made.

➤➤Step 15: Pause for Thought; Step 39: Listening Carefully; Step 40: How to Disagree; Step 41: Giving and Receiving Feedback; Step 46: Win-win Solutions

TECHNIQUE: The Anatomy of Conflict

Try these approaches to help you deal with conflict when it arises.

- Stay positive. Accept that conflict is an inevitable and necessary part of life.
- Determine whether you are facing actual conflict or just a perceived one. Many conflicts arise because one of the participants has made an assumption about the other that is inaccurate.
- Try to distinguish between helpful conflict (for example, when you are dealing with a difficult issue where there are no right or wrong answers and opposing viewpoints will generate new ideas) and unhelpful conflict (for example, where people's behaviour is causing aggressive responses).
- Watch out for early signs of conflict – for example, an aggressive stance, raised voices, over-defensiveness, unnecessary secrecy or open disagreement. Ensure that your own body language reinforces your point of view. For example, if you are trying to calm the situation, speak slowly and calmly and don't invade people's personal space.
- Try:

  listening to all sides and finding some common ground

  recognizing the feelings of other people

  focusing on the issues that really matter

  taking a break and coming back to the situation later

  using a neutral facilitator if you are in a seriously difficult conflict.

CHAPTER 9

Staying in Balance

American author Robert Fulghum suggested the following simple piece of advice: "Be aware of wonder. Live a balanced life – learn some and think some and draw and paint and sing and dance and play and work every day some."

If only it were so easy! But there is no doubt that being in balance is an important element of what you need to do to boost your mind. Otherwise all you are likely to achieve is a few moments of glory among much stress and inefficient working (and playing)! Whereas, if you can view everything from a balanced perspective, you are likely to keep on going when others fall by the wayside.

In this chapter you can asses how relaxed or stressed you are and find out how to get a grip on your life by concentrating on what really matters. You can also remind yourself of the importance of looking after yourself and invest some serious time with your nearest and dearest, planning your life.

48 Good Stress, Bad Stress

There is much talk of stress these days. Phrases and words like "stressed out", "stressy" and "de-stress" are everywhere. The almost universal view is that stress is a bad thing, something to be avoided. While prolonged exposure to stress is certainly bad for the mind and ultimately damaging to your immune system, some stress is not only inevitable but probably desirable.

For the mind to operate at its full potential, it requires a certain level of stress. As we learned in Step 6, it needs to be in a sufficient state of arousal, yet relaxed enough to concentrate. So it is more helpful to think in terms of good and bad stress.

Harnessed well, stress helps us through examinations, and allows us to excel at challenging intellectual assignments and endure physical hardship. When it is mismanaged it produces road rage or angry and rude behaviour. Too much stress, or extended periods of stress, stops your mind working at its full potential.

Managing stress

Stress in one area of life can spill over into other areas, until "my life is so stressful" becomes a general mantra that clouds the real issue. Unhelpful stress comes from predominantly two sources: people and situations. Try to identify who or what causes you to feel badly stressed. This will help you address the problem and work toward a solution or take avoidance measures.

Planning reduces stress considerably – just think how often you see other people (or yourself) boil over or fret because they've not left enough time for a journey or to prepare for something, or are confronted with something unexpected but (with hindsight) predictable. Imagine situations or confrontations and work through them in your mind so that you feel better prepared.

Physical health and mental calm are essential if stress is not to wear you down. Regular exercise helps, and yoga, autogenic training or meditation are beneficial, as are simple adjustments such as better sitting posture and controlled breathing.

Talk about things that are stressing you rather than bottling them up. To some people this comes naturally, but you may need to create the right circumstances. You could hold a regular family meeting, taking it in turns to share what's on each of your minds and offer help. You could ask everyone to share their favourite stress-busting tips and display these as posters at home or at work.

At the end of your working day, aim to wind down by using the last hour for the least stressful things – making some positive telephone calls, thinking about the next day or tidying up. When you arrive home, give yourself a few minutes of quiet reflection before you go through your front door.

Sleeping poorly makes stress less easy to cope with, and stress can make it difficult to sleep – a vicious circle. An evening walk or yoga session, supper with vivacious friends, the distraction of a good book or funny movie can all help you go to bed in a good, relaxed frame of mind.

At moments of stress, take slow, deep breaths. And take time out if you feel you need to, especially if you fear your judgment is being affected: just walk away, or busy yourself with something else or buy time under the guise of a comfort break.

To release pent-up stress, try keeping an old cushion or pillow to hand. Use it to take your frustrations out on. Pummel it, shouting out what's on your mind! Less dramatically, you could treat yourself to a massage. Humour can also be a great help. Keep a few DVDs/videos that are always guaranteed to make you laugh whatever your mood. Try to find something to laugh about in what you have just been through.

Use the checklist opposite to assess how well-balanced your life is. If the majority of your ticks end up in the two left hand columns of the chart, try to think of ways to redress the balance.

➤➤Step 5: Staying Healthy in Mind and Body; Step 6: Relaxed Alertness; Step 15: Pause for Thought; Step 35: Changing Behaviour; Step 47: Dealing with Conflict

CHECKLIST: **Is Your Life Well-balanced?**	Seldom	Sometimes	Very often	Always
Nine to fivers				
Do you get home from work before 7pm?				
Do you avoid working in the evenings?				
Do you avoid working at weekends?				
Are you relaxed when you get home?				
Other work styles				
If you work from home, do you stick to a reasonable cut-off time?				
If you work shifts do you manage to make space for your personal life?				
Home life				
If you are at home with young children, do you spend time with other adults?				
Do you have dinner with your partner?				
Social life and relaxation				
Do you see friends during the week?				
Do you fit hobbies or interests into your life?				
Do you take regular exercise?				
Do you wake up feeling refreshed and well-slept?				

49 Recharging Your Batteries

In Chapter 1 you learned about the importance of staying healthy and those principles remain important as you seek to stay in balance. But, from time to time, most of us find that our minds, like a run-down battery, need to be recharged.

A common idea for anyone who has been under stress is the need to take a break. This might involve lots of good sleeping, fresh air and a few stimulating but not over-taxing activities. But even down-time needs to be personalized. Just as we all learn in different ways, so we all recharge ourselves differently. Some people like to head for the hills and find solitude, while others seem to need the energy of others and would find a dinner party the perfect restorative.

Sometimes, though, what we think we need is not necessarily what is going to recharge us best. The old adage, "A change is as good as a rest," is a useful reminder that sometimes a contrast is precisely what we need. So, a gregarious person who enjoys regularly entertaining others might benefit from, say, a break at a meditation or yoga retreat, even if they don't feel that it's very "them". A reflective person who prays, reads and listens to music to unwind may benefit from, say, a weekend of group outdoor pursuits.

➤➤Step 5: Staying Healthy in Mind and Body; Step 24: What If?

EXERCISE: What Blend of Restoration Works for You?

This is an exercise in two parts. The easier, first part is coming up with ideas for recharging your batteries. The second part is to try to gauge more objectively what would be most effective for you.

Do you like to be:

- gregarious or solitary?
- indoors or outdoors?
- completely unplanned or with some planning?

Your answers may be a mixture of these. If so, what?

Do you want to (or might you want to) try:

- something contemplative, such as meditation, yoga or a retreat?
- a repetitive, mentally relaxing activity, such as jogging, walking or swimming?
- something else, such as a change of scenery? If so, what?

Combined, your answers should come up with your own personal recipe for a bit of mental (and physical) pampering. Now:

- compare it with your regular routine. Is it really different?
- ask your partner or a close friend what they think will work best for you (their answers to the questions above may result in a different recipe).
- let others know your plan so that they are aware of you needs and are able to offer encouragement and support.

50 How to Say No

Throughout this book I have stressed the importance of developing a positive mindset. So the idea of saying no may seem a surprisingly negative approach. But, as there are only so many hours in the day, it is actually one of the most important skills to learn. If you cannot say no, you will end up fretting more about others than you do about yourself and never having enough time to develop your own mind. You may also become unnecessarily dependent on others emotionally. And you are also likely to end up doing things that do not stretch your mind sufficiently.

By saying no to some things, you are effectively creating opportunities for your mind to explore other areas. Take a moment to reflect on your own life. Are there things you are currently involved in at home which, with hindsight, you should have said no to? And what about in your work life? Have you said yes to some things that are not really appropriate for you to be doing and do not offer you much stimulation?

It may be relatively easy to work out what you want to say no to, but extremely difficult to put it into practice. Indeed, some people go through their entire life allowing, as it were, people to trample over their own needs and aspirations by never sticking up for themselves. You do not want to be like this!

TECHNIQUE: **Refusing Gracefully**

Follow these three steps to help you develop an approach or approaches to saying no that will work for you.

1 Start by recognizing your feelings when you are asked to do something that you do not want to do. These could include: not wanting to hurt someone, worrying that the relationship will not work if you do not agree, fear that someone more powerful than you will like you less if you refuse to do something, even if they should be doing it for themselves. *Remember*: You are not responsible for other people's feelings!

2 Once you have recognized the feelings, stop and consider whether they are appropriate ones. Think carefully about the negative consequences if you do not say no. These could include: disappointing people if you fail to deliver and causing you stress as you try to do something you knew all along you could not or did not have time to do. *Remember*: You can stick up for yourself.

3 Just say *no*! This may be difficult if you normally say yes. So practise the exact form of words you might use. Be clear, honest and calm. *Remember*: People will respect you for being frank with them.

➤➤Step 16: Taking Stock; Step 47: Dealing with Conflict

51 Setting Goals

We might sometimes go for a drive just for fun, especially if we enjoy the thrill of a fast sports car, but mostly when we get in our car we have a definite destination in mind. So what about your life? Do you know where you are going? Do you have a clear set of goals?

Having clear goals is a sure way of boosting your mind power. To continue the car metaphor for a moment, can you remember how, when you or your family bought a new car, you suddenly started seeing lots of other cars of the same make on the road? This is because you will have shifted your focus of attention. Your mind has become interested in your particular type of car and starts to make the connection between others of the same kind.

The same thing happens with goals. If you work them out, set them and, ideally, write them down, your brain will start to focus on them. It will do this both consciously and unconsciously.

Of course, your ability to achieve your goals depends on what goals you actually choose. They need to be something you really want, not just something that sounds good or that you think you should want. At the same time it's no good setting entirely unrealistic goals. It's probably helpful to set a limited number of goals, with no more than one in each different area of your life (for example, work, home, health, personal development, relationships).

EXERCISE: What Are Your Aims?

Use the suggestions here to help you settle on some goals that are really important to you and how to work toward achieving them.

1 Take a moment to visualize yourself in five or 10 years' time. Close your eyes and picture what you will be doing, where you will be, who you will be with and how you will be feeling.
2 See if you can settle on no more than three goals. Think about your personal life. Think about your home. Think about work. Write down your goals in the form "I would like to..." For each one, be precise and realistic, aiming neither too high nor too low. Is one of your three goals more important than the others? If so, you might want to concentrate on that one alone to start with.
3 Now ask yourself how you are going to get there. Start to set yourself some short-term goals to help you achieve your larger, long-term goal(s), and give yourself a timescale, too. For example, if you want to emigrate to another country in five years' time, your short-term goals might include: This year: start learning the new language, devise a saving plan; Next year: plan an extended trip to research locations and familiarize yourself with the culture; The following year: investigate property prices, study local laws, and so on.

➤➤Step 19: Big and Small Pictures; Step 52: A Life Plan

52 A Life Plan

What is a typical day for you? Do you have plenty of time to do all the things you want to do or do you find, like most people, that time goes so fast that you frequently reach the end of the day exhausted but still with many of the things you hoped to achieve not done?

Without some prioritizing and planning, not just days but months and years can pass like this. But we have so much choice today and are surrounded by so much trivia. Put selfishly, if you want to boost your mind, then why waste your time doing things that do not matter and are unlikely to stretch you?

In Step 19 you learned about the value of thinking big and planning in smaller chunks. This is useful to have in the background as you draw up plans. Similarly, a well-tested question such as, Is it urgent and essential?, is a useful priority filter.

But for real mental development the questions you want to be able to answer yes to are: Will it challenge me? Is it difficult? Will I have to learn something new? Prioritizing for mind growth is different from prioritizing for an easy life! You need actively to look for opportunities for self-development. If you really want to boost your mind long-term, then you need a life plan.

I have developed the following approach to life planning, which I hope will be a helpful guide. It will encourage you to review the highs and lows of the previous year, think about what you want from life and how you are going to focus on getting more of it in the next twelve months. Finally, you will produce some kind of record of how and when you are going to do what you have decided.

Stage 1: Make time

This is not something to be squeezed into an evening between supper and bedtime. Set aside one whole weekend when you will not be disturbed by family or friends. Plan to do some of the things you most enjoy but leave lots of time to learn, feel and think.

You can spend this period alone or you might like to involve a close friend, so you can discuss ideas and support each other. If you have a partner, you will probably want to make a plan together as your lives are intertwined. Schedule in plenty of time to talk about your feelings, and discuss how you will help each other achieve your personal aims and how you will approach shared goals.

My wife and I find that the first weekend back in the real world after the summer holidays works well for us. We are relaxed and the world of work is a reality again but not an intrusive one. Grandparents or friends can often be persuaded to look after children to ensure that it is possible to have private time. In addition to finding time for this activity, it is also really important that you approach life planning with the right mindset and invest it with

100 percent effort. If you do not want to do it, it will not work. Similarly, if you or your companion's mind is elsewhere on other important things, you may struggle to make progress.

Stage 2: Make a start

Begin with the personal stuff and ask yourself some questions about your lifestyle, friendships and activities. To help review your year, you might look at some photographs or film of the past year or reflect on some particular items which carry special meaning for you. If you are doing this with your partner, then give each other private, quiet space at this stage, so that the initial thoughts and feelings you may later share are absolutely your own and not influenced by the other person. Here are some suggested questions for you to use as a starting point.

Home

- Are there aspects of your home environment which you would like to change?
- Which relationships do you invest most time in? Which *need* you invest most time in?
- Are you happy with your current circle of friends? Has it altered or stayed much the same?
- What kinds of books are you reading?

- What do you do in the way of hobbies or relaxation activities? Have you given up any or taken up something new?
- What exercise do you get? Have you given up anything or taken up something new?

At this stage you may like to think about some of the material things that are important to you – for example, jobs, careers, income, mortgages, and other practical considerations, but only after you have explored the personal stuff.

Work

- Do you find work stimulating and interesting, or boring?
- Do you feel you're being under-used, or struggling to do a good job?
- Has the nature of your work changed, or have you been doing much the same thing for years?
- Are you ambitious to get to the top of the ladder, or have you reached it?
- Are you anxious to make a major change?
- How are things on the financial front? Does this have a major bearing on your day-to-day life?

Think also about your highs and lows during the year. Then see if you can produce a list of "Things I would like to do more of" and "Things I would like to do less of".

Stage 3: Decide on a destination

Where do you go from here? Some short-term goals may be part of a longer-term plan, so think long term first. What are your ambitions? Do you want to work for ever? If you have a family, how may they figure in your future? It's a good idea to review steps 1 and 2 in the exercise on page 163 to remind yourself of some of the goals that you've already set, which are likely to feature in your plan.

Now turn your mind to the coming year. Think about what you are going to do, but on no account drift into the how at this point. Start with the big things, the principles, such as working shorter hours or spending more time with your most special friends, and then move on to think about the different areas of your life.

- What new learning opportunities could you create for yourself?
- What three things could you do to make your current job more interesting?
- Is there anything you would like to start studying?
- If you are happy with your circle of friends, what new things could you do to challenge you all? If not, how could you go about trying to meet new people with new ideas?

Draw up a list of headings from these kinds of words: Family, Our Partnership, Friends, Home, Garden, Holidays, Money, Health, Leisure, Spirituality and, of course, Boosting Your Mind. See if you can come up with one or two plans for each heading.

Stage 4: Reality check

If things have gone well for you in the past year, this is the most enjoyable part of the process. You may want to pick specific examples of things that you have definitely managed to achieve as a result of decisions you took. Taking stock like this makes you realize just how much of your life you can control. And just hearing yourself saying that you are going to stop doing some things and start doing others is intoxicating stuff! On the other hand, forever failing to reach your goals is dispiriting, so take a pause to consider the goals you have outlined for the coming year.

- Are they theoretically achievable or just pie in the sky?
- What are you doing to make them happen?
- Have you set a realistic timescale?

Step 5: Commit to a plan

It is psychologically very important that you actively commit yourself in words (and possibly pictures), to what you are going to do over the next year. It is also helpful to return to your plan several times during the year to see how things are going for you.

Many of the steps in this book have advice or exercises to help you achieve what you want, but in relation to the Life Plan, you might particularly like to review Step 16: Taking Stock, Step 35: Changing Behaviour, Step 36: Moving On and Step 51: Setting Goals.

Conclusion

The American management guru W. Edwards Deming, once said: "Learning is not compulsory, but neither is survival."

He was right. No one can force you to learn. You can, as it were, take a learner to water, but you cannot make her drink! But once you have started really trying to use your mind more effectively, you may well find that you are hooked. Like a wonderfully powerful and benign addictive drug, you will find that you want more and more. It is no exaggeration to say that boosting your mind power – learning in its broadest sense – is the key to unlocking your potential and to helping you to see things you have never noticed before. As award-winning author Doris Lessing put it: "This is what learning is. You suddenly understand something you've understood all your life, but in a new way."

The great thing about learning is that, not only does it equip you for survival, it also ensures that you feel better about yourself and stand a good chance of being happier and more successful in life. If you simply allow yourself to drift along always doing things in the same way, you may just about survive, but you are unlikely to thrive. Whereas if you are determined to see every experience and every mistake as a chance to do better next time around, then you are halfway to succeeding.

Further Reading

If you like my style, you may like to read these books, too:

Lucas, Bill *Discover Your Hidden Talents: the essential guide to lifelong learning,* Stafford, UK, 2005

Lucas, Bill *Power Up Your Mind: learn faster, work smarter*, Naperville, Illinois/London, 2001

Lucas, Bill and **Smith, Alistair** *Help Your Child to Succeed: the essential guide for parents*, Stafford, UK, 2002

Claxton, Guy and **Lucas, Bill** *Be Creative: essential steps to revitalise your work and life,* London, 2004

I recommend all these books, too:

Andreas, Steve and **Faulkner, Charles** *NLP: The New Technology of Achievement* (Audio), Fort Lauderdale, 1998/London, 1996

Butler, Gillian and **Hope, Tony** *Manage Your Mind,* Oxford, UK, 1995

Buzan, Tony *Use Your Head*, London, 2003

Claxton, Guy *Building Learning Power*, Bristol, UK, 2002

Claxton, Guy *Hare Brain, Tortoise Mind*, New York, 2000/London, 1998

Claxton, Guy *Wise Up: the challenge of lifelong learning*, New York/ London, 2000

Csikszentmihalyi, Mihalyi *Creativity: flow and the psychology of discovery and invention*, New York, 1997/London, 1996

Goleman, Daniel *Emotional Intelligence*, New York, 1997/London, 1996

Greenfield, Susan *BBC Brain Story: unlocking our inner world of emotions, memories and desires*, New York, 2001/*Brain Story: why do we think and feel as we do?*, London, 2000

Holford, Patrick *Optimum Nutrition for the Mind*, North Bergen, New Jersey, 2004/London, 2003

Honey, Peter and **Mumford, Alan** *The Learning Styles Questionnaire*, (Online), 1982

Langer, Ellen *The Power of Mindful Learning*, New York, 1997

Pert, Candace *Molecules of Emotion: why you feel the way you feel*, New York/London, 1999

Pinker, Stephen *The Blank Slate: the modern denial of human nature*, New York/London, 2002

Ratey, John *A User's Guide to the Brain*, New York, 2002/London, 2003

Robinson, Ken *Out of Our Minds: learning to be creative*, Oxford, UK, 2001

Rose, Colin and **Nicholl, Martin** *Accelerated Learning for the 21st Century: the six-step plan to unlock your master-mind*, New York/London, 1998

Seligman, Martin *Learned Optimism*, New York/London, 1998

Smith, Alistair *The Brain's Behind It: new knowledge about the brain and learning*, Stafford, UK, 2004

Sternberg, Robert *Successful Intelligence*, New York/London, 1997

Stoll, Louise et al *It's about Learning (and It's about Time)*, New York/London, 2002

Index

Contact the Author

If you would like to contact Bill Lucas, he can be reached through the following web address: www.bill-lucas.com

Author's acknowledgments

I would like to thank my wife and family for letting me try out many of these ideas on them! And Guy Claxton for his thinking and friendship.

Here is the answer to the puzzle on page 123.